art deco
architecture

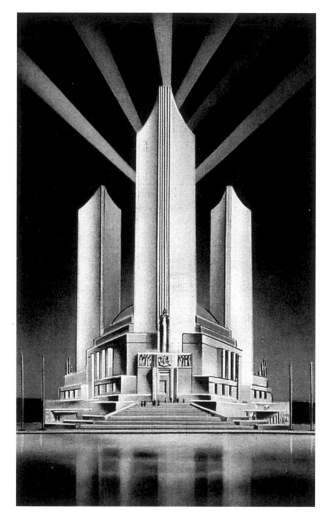

art deco
architecture
design, decoration and detail
from the twenties and thirties

Patricia Bayer

Harry N. Abrams, Inc., Publishers, New York

To Helen and James Bayer

Half-title: Three fluted towers around the dome of the
Federal Building, A Century of Progress exhibition, Chicago,
1933-34.

Frontispiece: Proscenium-shaped entrance to the Chrysler
Building, New York (William Van Alen, 1928-31).

Library of Congress Cataloging-in-Publication Data

Bayer, Patricia.
    Art deco architecture: design, decoration, and detail from the
twenties and thirties / by Patricia Bayer.
        p.   cm.
    Includes bibliographical references and index.
    ISBN 0–8109–1923–0
    1. Art deco (Architecture).   2. Decoration and ornament,
Architectural.   3. Architecture, Modern – 20th century.   I. Title.
NA682.A78B39 1992
724'. 6 – dc20
                                                    92–7342
                                                    CIP

Copyright © 1992 Thames and Hudson Ltd., London
Text copyright © 1992 Patricia Bayer

Published in 1992 by Harry N. Abrams, Incorporated, New York
A Times Mirror Company
All rights reserved. No part of the contents of this book may be
reproduced without the written permission of the publishers

Typeset by Litho Link Ltd, Welshpool, Powys, Wales
Printed and bound in Singapore

Acknowledgments

First and foremost, my thanks go to Frank Murphy for bearing with me
throughout the protracted duration of this project, which included extensive
photography as well as research and writing. Equal thanks go across the
Atlantic to my mother, Helen Bayer, who was a most agreeable and
enjoyable companion on my first trip to Miami Beach, and to my brother,
James Bayer, who accompanied me on visits to various Art Deco buildings in
Connecticut. I also want to single out and thank Martine de Cervens of
London for her constant support and ever willing-to-be-bent ear.
    In the United States, thanks are in order to a great many friends and
colleagues (some of whose names I will doubtless forget to mention), but
especially to Marian Appellof, who let me disrupt her life and flat for a few
autumn days in New York; Donna Cettei, who patiently and enthusiastically
acted as my chauffeur and hostess in Philadelphia and southern New Jersey;
Jacqueline Damian, who was a great sounding board and supporter; Barbara
Friedland, who put me up, put up with me and also photographed some
great buildings for me; and, as ever, to Michael Goldman, for providing me
with assorted reference books and long-distance support and encourage-
ment. Others I would like to thank are: in Connecticut, Michael Bingham
and Andrea Russo, Lorrie D'Apice, Diane Hart, William E. Keish of the
Connecticut Department of Transportation, Kathleen and David Mayhew,
Pamela Ross and Janet Zabicki; in New York, Valerie Cihylik, Jomarie DiIorio,
Sjoerd Doting, Victoria Horsman at N.W. Ayer, Howard and Ronald
Mandelbaum at Photofest, Althea McQueen at the Graybar Building, Albert
Paley, Cathy Peck, Jeffrey Pollock, Tony Walton and Roslyn Willett; in New
Jersey, Gloria and Ralph Cettei, the office of Michael Graves, and Steven C.
Wheatley; in Florida, Alice and Tim Doughty, Anita C. Gross of the
Wolfsonian Foundation, Sharon and David Lee, Mary and Henry Traskos,
and Cynthia and Robert Traskos, as well as assorted staff of the Miami
Design Preservation League; in Arizona, Barbara Worth and Sarah Suggs at
the Arizona Biltmore; in California, Maureen A. Kenney at Chevron, Pamela
Post at the University Art Museum, Santa Barbara, and two superb
photographers, Randy Juster in San Mateo and Julius Shulman in Los
Angeles; in Illinois, Katherine Hamilton-Smith at the Lake County Museum;
in Kentucky, Dale Curth of Arrasmith, Judd, Rapp, Inc.; in Ohio, Jeff Frank at
the Drexel, Columbus; in Oklahoma, John D. Bradley at the Boston Avenue
United Methodist Church and Robert Powers of the Tulsa Historical Society;
in Pennsylvania, Mort Blaustein, Sam Lambert and Peter B. Olson; in Texas,
June Griffin; in Virginia, Colleen Becker and Jim Schwan, Ashley Kistler and,
at Best Products, Ross Richardson; and in Washington, D.C., Gene Hertzog
of the Bureau of Reclamation, U.S. Department of the Interior.
    Also, thanks to Suzelle Baudouin at the Canadian Centre for Architecture,
Montreal; Peter Hallett of Napier, New Zealand, and Peter Thorn of the
Museum of Contemporary Art, Sydney. In Dublin, I would like to thank Sean
Rothery for his expert opinions and Tim Stuart for his extensive photographic
efforts, and in Cork, Tim O'Brien and Gareth O'Sullivan. Additional thanks
to Gea and Abdou el-Moutamid in Amsterdam; Malachy McCoy in
Barcelona; Ingo Schneeman in Frankfurt; Nicholas Law in Madrid; John
Carroll and Sylvette Gublin, Catherine Cheval, Ariane Garnier and especially
Patricia Hart in Paris; Lina Benassayag at the Hôtel Martinez, Cannes; and
Shin Takamatsu, Kyoto.
    In England, special thanks must go to Mark Waller, Catherine Littleton,
Marina van den Bosch et al. at Galerie Moderne, London, for the use of their
library and other help and suggestions. Also in London, I am grateful for
support and/or information from the following; Paul Anness, Valerie
Bennett at the Architectural Association, Derek Brampton at The Triangle
Bookshop, Mathilde Blum and Martin Morris, Gertrude Buckman, Niamh
Byrne at Unilever, Doug Cluett, Robert Cohen and Linda Sherrocks, June
Cook at the Ford Motor Company Ltd., David Coultas and Helen Ridge,
John Dorman and Eileen Vaughan, Allen Eyles, Jill Kristal Feuerstein, Rita
Fitzpatrick at the Australia High Commission, Julia Hawkins at Design
Analysis International Ltd., Warwick Hillman and Peter Scammell at the
Victoria Coach Station Ltd., Paul Lawson at London & Country (Green Line),
Joanna Lorenz, Stephen Luxford at the National Audit Office, Nancy
Mattson and Michael Shields, John McAslam, Deirdre O'Day, Derek
Penfold, Melissa Silcox at the Australian Tourist Commission, Sheila and
Dennis Simonds, Hony Snell at the Building Centre, Peggy Vance and, at
Indonesian Express, Khun Wijaya. Also in Great Britain, thanks to Christine
Clough, Sarah Henderson, Max R. Hagemann, Rob Mamuda and Bob
Warburton.
    Additional blanket thanks to the individuals, firms and organizations I am
sure I have managed to leave out above (but who may appear in the
Illustration Credits below).   **Patricia Bayer, London**

Contents

Chapter 1

Introduction

Art Deco architecture is a particularly hard concept to define; it refers to a decorative style at once traditional and innovative, which absorbed influences from a variety of sources and movements and introduced a whole range of new or improved materials into the vocabulary of architecture. In particular regions, idiosyncratic devices (such as tropical motifs in resort areas) were incorporated into the repertoire. Private, civic and ephemeral exhibition buildings in the Art Deco style appeared first in France, and foremost, a few years later, in the United States, as well as in a host of countries throughout the world. These structures were characterized by a mixture of materials and decorations, many recalling earlier forms. But the prime example of the Art Deco style in architecture was a distinctively urban construction: the exuberantly decorated, usually terraced, towering structure, epitomized by such Manhattan skyscrapers as the Chrysler and Empire State buildings. These lofty 'cathedrals of commerce' were largely made possible by developments in steel construction and reinforced concrete, integral components of most massive Art Deco edifices.

But besides these world-famous structures, Art Deco includes a myriad other orders of buildings, both vertical and horizontal, public and private, monumental and vernacular. Among these are blocks of Cubist-like apartment houses, massive power stations and factories, smoothly streamlined or colourfully exotic cinemas, ziggurat-form churches, and largely Neoclassical piles of interwar vintage, labelled Art Deco because of the stylized allegorical or floral reliefs (and often ornamental metalwork) which quietly yet strongly punctuate their exteriors. Some Art Deco buildings were stone-sheathed giants erected in the midst of older urban structures, while other, less oppressive and more modest commercial and residential edifices made up – and even defined – extensive areas. Included in this category would be a huge portion of the burgeoning resort of South Miami Beach, Florida, whose hotels and apartment complexes were designed in various, sometimes pastel-hued, permutations of a tropics-tinged Art Deco, and much of the town of Napier, New Zealand, destroyed by an earthquake in 1931 and subsequently largely rebuilt in the Art Deco mode.

Indeed, with their stylized floral panels and spandrels, their nicely curved streamlining, their Jazz Moderne or Zigzag Moderne (as it was sometimes called, especially in the nineteen-twenties) geometric elements, their handsome ornamental metalwork, their classical yet unmistakably modern

Opposite

Leonard Horowitz's colourful nineteen-eighties reconstruction of T. Hunter Henderson's 1930 MacArthur Hotel, Miami Beach, emphasizes the continuing fascination of the Deco style for architects and planners.

sculptures and reliefs, their generous use of colour (in terracotta ornament, metal, paint, stone and even stained glass) and their imaginative juxtaposition of light-and-dark and smooth-and-textured elements, Art Deco buildings appeared in many countries, leading one nineteen-twenties journal to call the style 'universalism'.

Simply because a building was erected in the interwar decades of the nineteen-twenties and nineteen-thirties, when Art Deco was at its zenith (especially in North America) does not, of course, justify its being called Art Deco. Neither does the addition of a single sunburst door or window design on an otherwise provincial, mock-Tudor row house in the London suburbs, for example – although that motif without doubt is considered quintessential Art Deco. Undecorated, largely concrete structures in the Bauhaus, Modernist, Modern Movement or International School vein are often simply called Art Deco because of their boxy, rectilinear shapes, but the lack of any outstanding ornament, polychromy, distinctive lettering or ornamental metalwork generally disqualifies them from being classified under the Art Deco rubric, at least in the eyes of purists.

Essentially, it should be remembered that the Art Deco style is generally applied to the decorative or applied arts and not to architecture as such, the way there was an Amsterdam School, Prairie School, Italian Futurism, Finnish National Romanticism and the Bauhaus. The architects, especially the Americans, who designed what are now identified as Art Deco buildings, were on the whole classically trained; their creations were traditional in terms of their inner structures, materials and services. Steel skeletons and reinforced-concrete elements were by the nineteen-thirties the norm, and not innovatory. What made the buildings Art Deco was not their sheer height; extremely tall buildings had already been erected at the turn of the century in both New York and Chicago. It was their generally non-structural decorative elements and, in the case of Manhattan and other big-city buildings, their set-back, terraced silhouettes (which were in fact necessitated by a legal zoning requirement imposed in 1916 by city authorities so that the soaring structures would not rob the streets and people below of light and air) which defined their style. We are, then, concerned here essentially with surface and form.

Art Deco architecture was an architecture of ornament, geometry, energy, retrospection, optimism, colour, texture, light and at times even symbolism; many times this vibrant, decorative interwar architectural style was marked by a lively, altogether unexpected, interaction and contrasting of two or more of these elements. It is interesting to note that there were far more public than private buildings designed in the Art Deco style. More than anything, Art Deco was an architecture of soaring skyscrapers – the cathedrals of the modern age – and decorated, not at all depressing, civic and residential structures. It was at once an official, vernacular and fugitive architecture, encompassing, respectively, monumental, yet exuberantly ornamented, city halls, schools and post offices, gleaming roadside diners and streamlined dry cleaners, and fantastic world fair pavilions.

Chas. Heathcote & Sons designed this jazzy London doorway (c.1930) (*opposite above*) for the Ford showroom in Regent Street; the metal greyhounds at the upper sides were popular Deco-era images of speed. Several years earlier in Manhattan, the 1923-26 Barclay-Vesey (or New York Telephone) Building, one of the city's earliest skyscrapers, featured interlacing tendrils (*opposite below*) that related to an earlier (i.e. Art Nouveau) period (see page 105 for a full view). Note the bell in the central panel, the telephone company symbol. Ralph T. Walker designed the building for the firm McKenzie, Voorhees & Gmelin.

Overleaf

A wealth of Art Deco details – floral, geometric, figurative and exotic (*from the top, left to right*): a house in Vaison-la-Romaine, Provence; floral panel, Polish National Home, Hartford, Connecticut; polychrome Pueblo Deco decoration, New York apartments, East 22nd Street; The Surfcomber, Miami Beach; Moderne typeface on keystone panel of Evelyn apartments, Miami Beach; office skyscraper, 500 Fifth Avenue, New York; Native American motifs on the KiMo Theater, Albuquerque; News Building, New York; floral garland, Paris apartment building, 20 Avenue du Président Kennedy; commercial building, upper Broadway, New York; Lasher Printing Company, Philadelphia; and Beneficial Savings Bank, North Broad Street and Chew Avenue, Philadelphia.

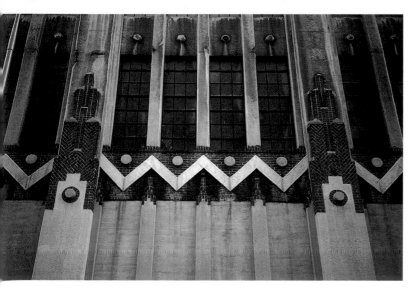

Art Deco followed and coexisted with a number of other styles, many of whose characteristics it sometimes shared: the straight lines of the Modern Movement, Bauhaus, Rationalism, De Stijl and the International Style, and the decorative, highly sculptural elements of the Viennese Secession, Dutch Expressionism (seen at its best in the creations of the Amsterdam School), Scandinavian Romanticism and Neoclassicism, British Arts and Crafts, the Chicago School and Frank Lloyd Wright's successive Prairie School, and even its highly organic immediate precursor, Art Nouveau or Jugendstil. Many creators of Art Deco buildings absorbed the styles of the ancient past as well, imbuing them with an undeniable sense of modernism. This was not the modernism we attribute today to the International Movement, but 'modernism' as the term was more simply applied in the nineteen-twenties and nineteen-thirties meaning something new and different, something exciting and unorthodox, something characterized by a sense of *joie de vivre* that manifested itself in terms of colour, height, decoration and sometimes all three.

Art Deco is in fact a relatively recent term, coming into general usage soon after a 1966 exhibition, 'Les Années "25" Art Déco/Bauhaus/Stijl/ Esprit Nouveau', presented at the Musée des Arts Décoratifs, Paris. 'Art Deco' derived directly from the 1925 Exposition des Arts Décoratifs et Industriels Modernes in Paris, the exciting world fair that was in fact the high point of the French *moderne* style and the starting-off point for American adaptations and offshoots of it.

Art Deco architecture is not an architecture of personalities, of star architects. It is an architecture of the buildings themselves, of their inherent yet overt qualities and of their spirit, energy and immediate visual impact, not of their internal structures, services, floor plans, and front and side elevations. Few members of the general public in the West can name an Art Deco architect, but most are more than familiar, for instance, with the Empire State Building.

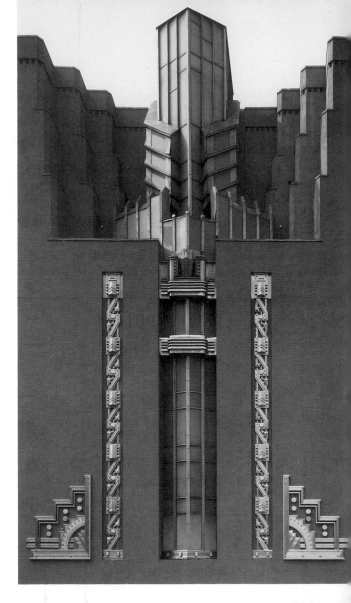

The form of Harry Sternfeld and Gabriel Roth's WCAU Building (*right above*) in Philadelphia was meant to represent a radio wave (the 1928 structure's lower section can be seen on page 91). During nocturnal radio broadcasts, a blue light glowed from the glazed parapet. The stepped form of the Pennsylvania structure is echoed in the terracotta decoration adorning a commercial building in 345 Hudson Street, Manhattan (*right*).

The exterior of Ely Jacques Kahn's 2 Park Avenue Building (*opposite*), at 32nd and 33rd streets, New York, was covered with the architect's distinctive, heavy-metal cladding. It was designed in 1927 when the architect was a partner in Buchman & Kahn.

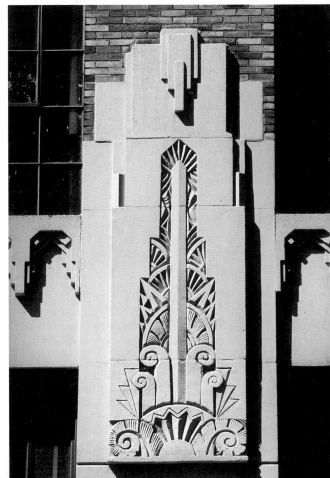

12

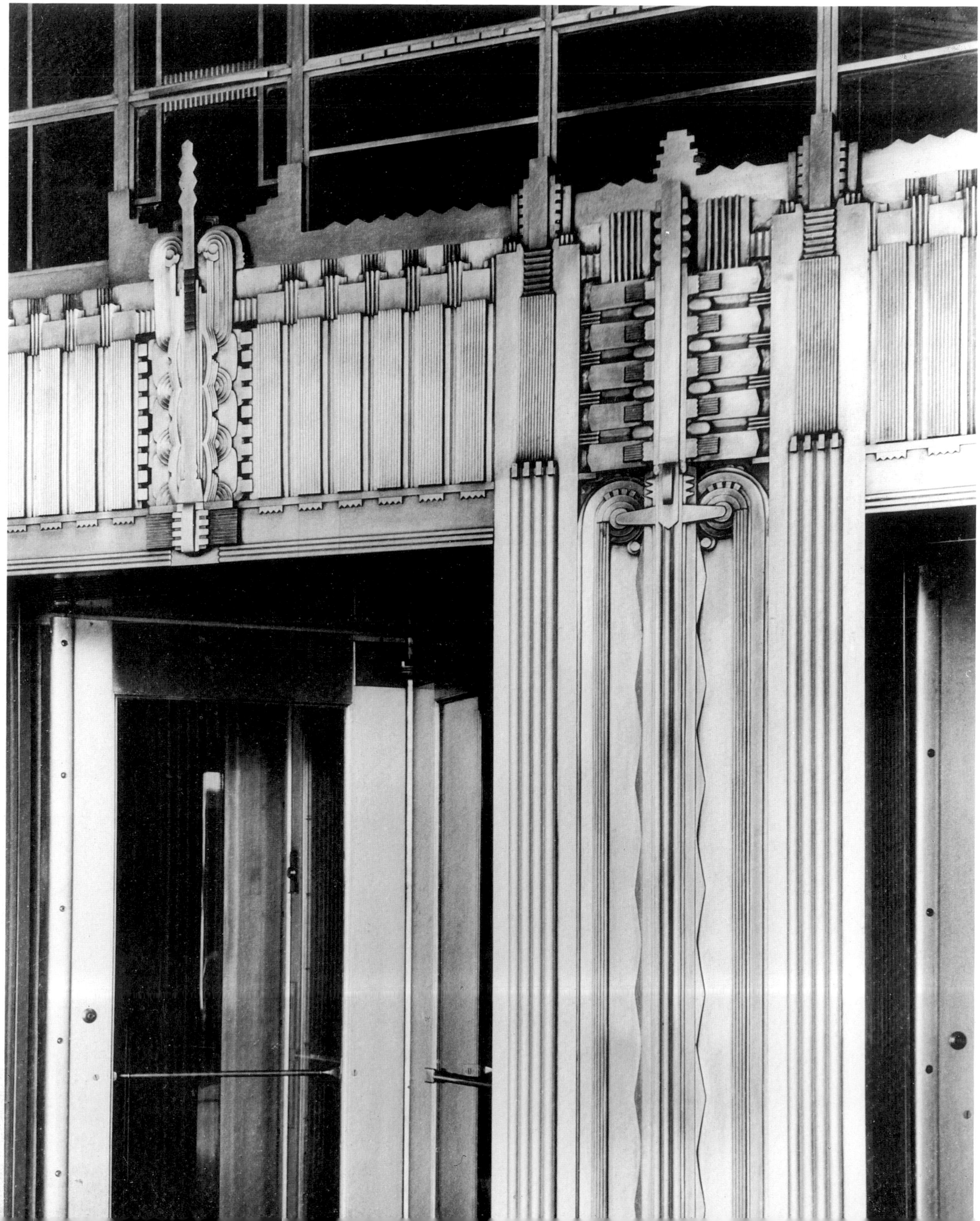

Chapter 2

Influences, Precursors and Parallels

Two views of Ideal House or the National Radiator Building, London (now Palladium House), designed by Raymond M. Hood and Gordon Jeeves, 1928: a romantic rendering by Lawrence Stone (*opposite*) from *The Architectural Review*, June 1929, and a detail of the upper corner (*above*). One of London's jazziest Moderne buildings, this confection was clad in black granite and highlighted with Moorish- and Persian-inspired enamel-on-bronze decoration by the Birmingham Guild of Handicraft.

Just as the Art Deco style in the applied arts was an eclectic hybrid, drawing inspiration from international sources as disparate as tribal African sculpture, the Ballets Russes, Japanese lacquerwork and Mayan temples, so Art Deco architecture was informed by a variety of ancient, exotic and more recent sources.

The discovery of Tutankhamun's treasure-laden tomb in the Valley of Kings by Howard Carter in 1922 inspired yet another fashion for things Egyptian. This time, however, Egyptian-influenced buildings and objects were often created – on both sides of the Atlantic – in *le style moderne*, duly conventionalized in a manner that both acknowledged their inspiration and boldly asserted the period in which they were fashioned. An Egyptian-style Art Deco building could take on, or more usually, be topped by, a pyramid, or its façade could assume the look of an Egyptian temple, such as London's Karnak-inspired Carlton Cinema in Essex Road (George Coles, 1930) and Wallis, Gilbert & Partners' early nineteen-thirties Hall & Co. Building and India Tyre Factory, in London and Inchinnan, Scotland, respectively. Generally, however, Egyptian elements, including stylized lotus blossoms, scarabs and papyrus leaves, were used in tandem with other exotic motifs, on cinemas and numerous civic and public structures, such as the Los Angeles Public Library.

The decorative motifs of the ancient Near Eastern cultures of Assyria, Babylonia and Sumer also inspired some Art Deco architects, mainly in sculptural decoration. The former Pythian Temple in West 70th Street, New York, features polychrome Near Eastern details, and the old Samson Tyre and Rubber Company (recently reincarnated as The Citadel, a factory-outlet shopping precinct) in Los Angeles is essentially a massive neo-Assyrian palace.

Occasionally, stylized Persian or Moorish details appear on Art Deco buildings, a fine example being the former Ideal House, or National Radiator Building (now Palladium House) in London, termed 'The Moor of Argyll Street' in the June 1929 issue of *The Architectural Review*, which featured the new building by Raymond M. Hood and Gordon Jeeves.

For centuries the classical structures and sculpture of Greece and Rome inspired – were indeed the fountainhead of design for – later architects, and the early twentieth century was no different. But Art Deco architects were in part reacting against what had become the norm of Beaux-Arts Neoclassicism, so they added distinctively Moderne (or simply modernized) elements to their classically based creations: stylized eagles and blossoms, bold sunrays, strings of zigzags, characters in contemporary dress on bas-relief panels. As in other periods, figures from classical mythology proved popular subjects on Art Deco buildings, from the numerous polychrome reliefs and gilded statues scattered around New York's Rockefeller Center to the friezes adorning the Théâtre des Champs-Elysées in Paris.

Aspects of medieval and Byzantine architecture also found their way into Art Deco buildings, from the neo-Romanesque 1931-36 church of Sacré-Coeur in Gentilly, just outside Paris, whose tower is dominated by four angels of quasi-Moderne mien and whose tympanum sculptures are in a similar mode, to the steel eagle gargoyles, resolutely aiming outwards like giant hood ornaments against the sky, on New York's Chrysler Building.

The influence of the Mayan and Aztec and Native American cultures, largely confined to the New World, was manifested in a variety of early twentieth-century buildings in the United States, Canada and Mexico. The Mexican Revolution, which began in 1910, further spread the appeal of traditional styles and motifs, namely, stepped pyramids (such as those at Chichen Itza and Uxmal), deities in elaborate headdresses and costumes, stylized sunrays (a device used in many cultures throughout time) and dense patterns of circles, snakes, curlicues and geometric shapes. In fact, the Mayan Revival style began to evolve a decade or so earlier than Art Deco, making it less a subcategory of the larger style and more a self-sufficient though not entirely separate movement. Certain aspects of Pre-Columbian art, design and architecture were altered or updated by architects, such as Robert B. Stacy-Judd in California, to fit the taste of the nineteen-twenties and nineteen-thirties, thus making them a part of the extensive, eclectic Art Deco vocabulary.

Native American motifs were also adapted by Art Deco architects and used to decorate public buildings, especially in the American South and West and in parts of Canada. Symbols like the Hopi bird and Navajo stepped cloud appeared on train stations, hotels, city halls and a host of other buildings in the United States, while in northern Canada totem-pole pilasters and Indian beadwork motifs adorned banks and public libraries.

The rectangular adobe structures of Pueblo tribes of the American Southwest – the only native Americans to produce permanent architecture – were the inspiration for some modern buildings in that part of the United States. Western praise, and preservation, of these traditional structures came about largely through the efforts of artists' communities in Taos and Santa Fe, New Mexico, one of whom pointed out in 1923 that 'the Indians were the first Cubists in this country'. The buff, pink and even blue tones of adobe were replicated in more durable stucco and plaster from the nineteen-twenties, and these largely rectilinear structures, from private houses to hospitals, related both to Native American antecedents and modern European contemporaries.

An important lateral influence on Art Deco was industrial design, a purely twentieth-century phenomenon whose American exponents – Raymond Loewy, Norman Bel Geddes and Walter Dorwin Teague foremost among them – not only held great sway over others in their field, but whose revolutionary ideas and products spread out to other disciplines, including architecture. The strong, often streamlined, forms of industrial design informed many a commercial structure in the nineteen-thirties, and in fact the designers themselves turned their hands to creating actual buildings: Teague built filling stations, Bel Geddes world fair pavilions and Loewy bus terminals. There are even quasi-whimsical but altogether functional examples of new and improved industrially designed products metamorphosing into buildings. Among these are photographic-supply shops with camera façades, refrigerator-crowned and -shaped stepped structures serving as showrooms for the popular new appliance (respectively, Raymond Hood's buildings for Rex Cole in Brooklyn and Queens, New York), Alfonso Iannelli's giant Havoline Thermometer crowning that company's building at the 1933-34 Century of Progress Exposition in Chicago and Walter Dorwin Teague's National Cash Register Company pavilion at the 1939-40 New York World Fair, surmounted by a giant cash register whose numbers tallied up fair attendance. Other examples scattered across the United States include a Moderne teapot-shaped snack bar.

The large ocean-going vessel, an integral part of nineteen-twenties and nineteen-thirties travel, inspired Art Deco buildings of the Streamline Moderne variety. Perhaps the best-known example of borrowing is Robert V. Derrah's 1936-37 design for the Coca-Cola Bottling Company building in Los Angeles, with its portholes, promenade deck, ship's bridge and numerous other maritime details (the company chairman had a keen interest in ships). Elsewhere throughout the world, especially in tropical coastal areas, nautical motifs appeared in profusion. Even in inland Australia, the so-called Modern Ship Style shone in what is probably that country's finest example of Art Deco residential architecture, Burnham Beeches in Sherbrooke, Victoria (Harry Norris, 1933).

Not surprisingly, many of the immediate stylistic precursors of Art Deco, some of which in fact overlapped the style, had a considerable impact on the buildings of the nineteen-twenties and nineteen-thirties. Art Deco did not, after all, emerge out of thin air or as a deliberate reaction to another style. Rather, it evolved quietly from the pre-First World War period, seeing its apotheosis in the 1925 Paris Exposition, and afterwards gaining second-wind momentum, albeit in a filtered down, multi-faceted guise, in other countries, especially the United States.

Of the many schools and movements in *fin-de-siècle* European architecture, that espoused by members of the so-called Vienna Secession was the closest in terms of style to the later Art Deco style. Foremost among the Secession projects was the lavish Palais Stoclet, a private house built in Brussels from 1905 to 1910 to a design by Josef Hoffmann, one of the founders of the Wiener Werkstätte (whose members largely furnished the house, along with contributions by Secession artist Gustav Klimt). The Palais Stoclet was at once Neoclassical and contemporary, a low, rectilinear structure of white marble embellished with elaborate bronze sculpture and floral decorations. It foresaw both the no-nonsense, white-box International Style and ornamented Art Deco, while occupying a pedestal all its own in early twentieth-century architectural terms.

More than any other British structures, the creations of Charles Rennie Mackintosh — the Glasgow School of Art foremost among them — look forward to aspects of Art Deco, especially in colour, texture and stylized decoration in stone, metalwork and glass. Likewise, traces of the distinctive conventionalized leaf and other organic devices used by architects and designers of the Arts and Crafts Movement in Britain (and the United States) can occasionally be discerned in fantastic species of Art Deco flora (for example, some of the bas-reliefs adorning the 1930 Southern New England Telephone Company building in Hartford).

In 1914-16 in Manchester, England, Edgar Wood designed and had built for himself Royd House, an unusual brick residence whose concave front elevation, with a bold zigzag design over the door that almost reached to the roof line, has been called by design historian Bevis Hillier 'a visionary building . . . the most striking single precursor of Art Deco'. Also in the spirit of the future were some German turn-of-the-century structures built in the Jugendstil mode. Austrian Joseph Maria Olbrich's long, low Ernst Ludwig House at Mathildenhöhe, the artists' colony set up from 1900 to 1907 near Darmstadt by Grand Duke Ernst Ludwig of Hesse, features striking decoration at the entrance: two huge human figures and, behind them, bronze angels. The most dramatic building in the complex is Olbrich's Hochzeitsturm (Wedding Tower), whose five-part stepped roof — apparently intended to represent a raised hand — foreshadows later skyscrapers.

An important Parisian precedent of the Art Deco style dates from the Art Nouveau period, although it is far from curvilinear: Auguste Perret's transitional 1902-4 Rue Franklin apartment building, an example of French Rationalism that was revolutionary in its reinforced concrete frame and extensive glazing. Perret's structure is significant in relation to Art Deco for its profuse decoration, characterized not by the snaking foliage of Art Nouveau, but more by stylized flowers and dense circular patterns, designed by Alexandre Bigot and moulded on to large *grès* ceramic tiles. Though these did not directly prefigure the stylized blossoms and geometric ornament of Art Deco, nonetheless their designs serve as a bridge between the organic veracity of Art Nouveau and a more ordered floral fantasy of Art Deco.

Another Continental movement with roots in the early twentieth century and branches extending to Art Deco (as well as to the International Style) was Expressionism, in both its German and Dutch manifestations. This eclectic anti-historicizing architectural style, which found its initial expression a decade or so before the First World War but flourished in the nineteen-twenties, was a logical progression from Jugendstil. Peter Behrens' monumental glass and steel turbine factory of 1908-9, for the Allgemeine Elektrizitätsgesellschaft (German General Electric Company) provided inspiration, if not a model, for many Art Deco-era factories. Equally significant were the decorative brick-clad water tower and exhibition hall (1911) in Poznán, Poland, by Hans Poelzig, and two later structures: the futuristic Einstein Tower (1917-21) at Potsdam, by Erich Mendelsohn, and the sharp upwards-thrusting, elaborately decorated Chilehaus (1922-23), Fritz Höger's Berlin masterpiece.

In contrast to the mainly industrial structures which came to define German Expressionist architecture, Dutch Expressionism's Amsterdam School found its best expression in handsome brick buildings, including low-cost housing in that city. A plethora of sculptural and other decorative elements abounded in these vibrant structures, whose principal creators were Johan Melchior van der Mey, Michel de Klerk and Piet Lodewijk Kramer (who were largely influenced by Hendrik Berlage and the young Frank Lloyd Wright). Besides the various residential structures created by the three main figures, significant Amsterdam School structures included the Scheepvaarthuis office building (1911-16), a collaborative effort of the three which housed a half dozen major shipping firms and whose densely decorated façade contained sculptural references to the sea, and Kramer's De Bijenkorf (The Beehive) department store in The Hague (1924-25), which could easily be called Art Deco with its curved elements, relief sculptures and harmonious combination of brick, glass and concrete. De Klerk designed a fantastic but unrealized high-rise in 1920.

One structure that was to inspire (indirectly) American architects of the nineteen-twenties and thirties was Eliel Saarinen's 1904-14 Railway Station in Helsinki, which is at once a manifestation of Art Nouveau, Neoclassicism and National Romanticism. Its four monumental figures by Emil Wikstrom, two each astride the main entrance arch, relate to both contemporaneous Viennese structures and later Art Deco skyscrapers, and the masterful stone massing and streamlined details presage later such monumental travel-related structures.

Italian Futurist architecture was dominated by Antonio Sant'Elia, virtually none of whose projects was ever realized (he left behind over 300 powerful, visionary drawings after his death in the First World War). Influenced by Italian Art Nouveau (Stile Liberty) architects, as well as the Vienna Secession and early American skyscrapers, Sant'Elia evolved his own futuristic architectural vocabulary, much as did Hugh Ferriss, the New York architect-draughtsman whose spectacular creative projects existed only on paper. Massive terraced structures, dizzying loops of roadways, slim concrete and steel spans and other grand, ultimately romantic, elements comprised Sant'Elia's utopian conurbations. His one quasi-realized project, the 1933

War Memorial at Como, was built belatedly, in a simplified version, under the supervision of International Style architect Giuseppe Terragni.

The Chicago School of architecture, guided by Beaux-Arts-trained Henry Hobson Richardson and, later, by Louis Sullivan, flourished from around 1875 to 1910, creating large-scale office and other commercial steel-skeleton structures which were above all functionalist in nature. Unlike the early Chicago School creations, the *fin-de-siècle* examples embraced rather than eschewed decoration, and it was this ornament, as well as the sheer vertical massiveness of many of these structures, that left a mark and duly inspired architects working on large commercial projects in the Moderne nineteen-twenties and thirties.

An important precursor of the decorated proto-modern oversized structure was Louis Sullivan's Schlesinger and Mayer Department Store (completed in 1904), today Carson Pirie Scott & Co., a twelve-storey Chicago emporium whose façade stood proud, even dazzled, with an overall gridwork pattern of horizontals and verticals (echoing the steel skeleton below it), wide, deeply recessed windows and, especially, a dense florid design in terracotta sheathing the store's two lower floors. Sullivan proved that decoration and functionalism could comfortably coexist in a commercial building.

The many, diverse creations of Louis Sullivan's most gifted student, Frank Lloyd Wright, cut across a number of late nineteenth- and twentieth-century architectural styles, as well as creating several new swathes (and schools) on their own. Without doubt, Wright's 1914 Midway Gardens in Chicago, a restaurant/amusement park complex with profuse sculptural decoration, was a harbinger of Art Deco (sadly, it was demolished in 1929). Some Wright structures have even been termed Art Deco (which may be anathema to Wright scholars and purists), such as the early nineteen-twenties Mayan-inspired textile-block houses in California, the Imperial Hotel in Tokyo (1915-22) and the Johnson Wax Administration Building in Racine, Wisconsin (1936-39).

Architectural movements and schools contemporary with Art Deco included styles both fiercely antithetical to it and nicely paralleling it. However, even in buildings created in the former styles, there could be found certain unmistakable affinities with Art Deco: a subtle streamlined or geometric element, perhaps, or an otherwise discreet concession to ornament.

Foremost among the contemporaries of Art Deco which marched decidedly to a different drum were the exponents of the non-revivalist Cubist-inspired Modern Movement, or International Style, as architectural historian Henry-Russell Hitchcock first called it in 1929, which was initially championed by mainly European architects. Hitchcock numbered among these 'New Pioneers' the French architects Le Corbusier and André Lurçat, Dutchmen J.J.P. Oud and Gerrit Rietveld, and Germans Walter Gropius and Mies van der Rohe. To this list could be added Eileen Gray, Marcel Breuer, Rudolph Schindler and Richard Neutra, two Austrians who emigrated to the

In 1914 Frank Lloyd Wright designed Midway Gardens, a sprawling Chicago entertainment complex that provided the public with handsome space for numerous activities, including dining, dancing and listening to music. Roman brick and cast concrete blocks decorated with geometric patterns were used for the park's diverse structures, which can be seen as harbingers of the Art Deco style in the United States; the park was demolished in 1929.

United States, the Viennese Adolf Loos, who lived in Paris from 1923 to 1928, the Finn Alvar Aalto, the Italian Giuseppe Terragni and British-based Berthold Lubetkin, Wells Coates, Maxwell Fry, Serge Chermayeff and, from 1933 to 1939, before he moved to the United States, Erich Mendelsohn. Robert Mallet-Stevens — a French architect whose formal, Cubist-influenced, but often subtly ornamented, buildings are referred to by most experts as Art Deco, but by others as Modernist — is that *rara avis* whose hybrid structures contain salient elements of both styles.

The large body of buildings designed by Le Corbusier (Charles-Edouard Jeanneret) (1887-1965) best illustrate the strengths, and indeed the timeless nature (as we now view it in retrospect), of the straight-edged, pared-down, volume- rather than mass-orientated Modern Movement (or Purism, as the architect called it). Although not the first example of this flexible, largely pure-white aesthetic style, a significant structure in terms of this book is Le Corbusier's L'Esprit Nouveau pavilion at the 1925 Paris Exposition, a prototype for a mass-manufactured 'machine à habiter' which was named after the radical art journal (1920-25) the architect founded with Amédée Ozenfant.

Later Modernist buildings did not seem as severe and 'purist', probably because they were actual, lived-in structures, which could be viewed in practical terms and in direct relation to their setting. Irish-born Eileen Gray's so-called E-1027 (1927), a cliffside, white-washed Riviera dwelling designed for her and Jean Badovici, blended in with, rather than overpowered, its magnificent setting. On the other hand, Le Corbusier and Pierre Jeanneret's Villa Savoye in Poissy-sur-Seine (1929-31), derided as a 'box on stilts' by Frank Lloyd Wright, seems an incongruous, even alien, cube suspended on *pilotis* and inhabiting a flat, rural locale.

Other simple Modernist 'boxes' and multi-cubed structures made strong, positive statements throughout the world, from Athens to Zürich, from New York to New South Wales, from Plumstead to Prague. Because unlike the typical Art Deco building, which is a large public structure, the quintessential Modernist creation is small and residential. However, such Streamline Moderne elements as bullnose balconies, curved railings and porthole windows appear often on fundamentally Modernist creations, leading many to call them Art Deco. This misses the point that ornament and to a lesser extent colour are the most characteristic features of Art Deco architecture.

Notwithstanding that fact, there is no mistaking Gerrit Rietveld's Schröder House in Utrecht (1924) for Art Deco. As with the primary-hued canvases of De Stijl painter Piet Mondrian, the strictly rectilinear Utrecht house is white with red, blue, yellow and black highlights, both inside and out. It is supremely functionalist and practical, and bereft of any extraneous decoration, other than colour. The house is an icon of Dutch De Stijl, a style that was decidedly antithetical to the humanist Amsterdam School, which embraced ornament – even whimsy – on residential and commercial buildings alike. The Amsterdam School's buildings more or less spanned the same years as Art Deco (its review, *Wendingen*, existed from 1918 to 1936) but, unlike rectilinear Modernism, they were not at odds with their decorative French counterparts; indeed, they complemented them and provided inspiration to Art Deco architects abroad.

Another Dutch architect, Willem Marinus Dudok (1884-1974), deserves mention. Though not formally allied with the two above-named schools, he was not oblivious to their output. Over his two-decades-long tenure as, first, director of municipal works (1915-27) and then town architect at Hilversum, Dudok evolved his own distinctive civic style, which proved highly influential abroad, especially in England. Like several buildings created by his Expressionist compatriot, Michel de Klerk, Dudok's work – notably his 1928-30 Raadhuis (Town Hall) in Hilversum – comprised massive brick forms which achieved a lightness and even warmth in their pleasing juxtaposition of verticals and horizontals and their frequent use of light-coloured brick.

The Bauhaus thrived in Germany from 1919 to 1933, after which time other European countries and the United States benefited from the talents of many of its teachers and students. Informed by such movements as Arts and Crafts, De Stijl and Russian Constructivism, all of which encouraged the collaborative efforts of artists, designers and architects, the Bauhaus did not in fact have an architecture department until 1927. However, the Bauhaus's founding director (until 1928), Walter Gropius — whose first important building was the massive steel-and-glass Fagus Factory of 1911 — had designed a complex of functionalist school buildings at Dessau, where the 'campus' moved from Weimar in 1925. Residential structures by Bauhaus architects, such as Mies van der Rohe's Tugendhat House in Brno (1930), related chiefly to French and other European Modernist counterparts.

Among the Russian architects working in the twenties and thirties the foremost was Konstantin Melnikov, whose double-cylindrical design for his own Moscow house (1927), punctuated with myriad hexagonal windows, was a fascinating model of Modernism. More Cubist but equally dramatic was his Rusakov Club (1927-28), one of a series of five workers' clubs in Moscow: its salient feature was a trio of cantilevered classroom-boxes which extended outwards from the top storey of the building.

In Prague and elsewhere in Czechoslovakia, a short-lived design movement called Czech Cubism began in 1911, with architects Josef Gočár, Vlastislav Hofman and Pavel Janák among its exponents. As with sculptor Raymond Duchamp-Villon's experimental Villa Cubiste (1912), the Cubist elements of the Czech structures largely comprised undistinguished building forms marked by the angular ornamentation on their façades. In this respect they foreshadowed a good many Parisian apartment blocks of the nineteen-twenties, whose overall shapes were indistinguishable from late nineteenth-century Beaux-Arts buildings, but whose decoration (grillework, bas-reliefs and other sculptural elements) was unmistakably Moderne.

Large-scale Neoclassical, neo-Byzantine and neo-Gothic buildings, usually of a civic nature, continued to be built throughout the world in the nineteen-twenties and nineteen-thirties. We can note the following as supreme examples of historical styles: the neo-Byzantine Australian War Memorial in Canberra (John Crust & Emil Sodersten, 1941), Edwin Lutyens' Viceroy's House in New Delhi (1912-31), the 30th Street Station in Philadelphia (Graham, Anderson, Probst & White, 1929-34) and the Supreme Court of Canada in Ottawa (Ernest Cormier, 1938-39).

On the other side of the world, several disillusioned students at Tokyo Imperial University boldly rejected the traditional architecture of their country in 1920 and formed the Japanese Secession, which took much of their initial inspiration from European Expressionism. Some of their radical (in Oriental terms) projects could be said to have an affinity with Art Deco as well, such as Mamoru Yamada's Central Telegraph Office in Tokyo (1926), with its elliptical arches and overall futurist bent, and later buildings like Tetsuo Yoshida's General Post Office in Tokyo (1931), a massive box with a decidedly Modernist aspect.

The architecture of ancient Egypt was one of several sources of Art Deco design, but in fact that culture held a perennial appeal for Europeans, with Egyptian Revival buildings appearing from the Renaissance onwards. The 1828 engraving of London's Egyptian Hall, Piccadilly (*left*), dates from a spate of 'Egyptomania' spurred on by Napoleon's North African battles.

At the 1893 World Columbian Exposition in Chicago, the 'Golden Door' to Louis Sullivan's Transportation Building (*below*) was a dazzling, eccentric and indeed modern statement among a sea of sombre Neoclassical pavilions.

The stepped pyramid of ancient Meso-America such as the palace at Xpuhil, Mexico (*right*), was a building type adapted and updated frequently in American Art Deco.

These renderings of Dutch Expressionist buildings by Michel de Klerk were harbingers of Art Deco skyscrapers: a 1915 competition design for a high-rise building (*left*) and a 1912 competition entry for a reinforced-concrete water tower (*below right*).

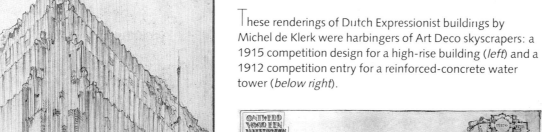

Auguste Perret's 1902-4 apartment house on 25 bis Rue Franklin (*above left*) is an early reinforced concrete-framed building, although its terracotta sheathing and dense floral 'coverage' – a precursor of profuse florid Art Deco details – help give equal weight to its decoration and structure. The startlingly futuristic nineteen-twenties design by Perret (*below left*) was for suburban Paris tower blocks, never-realized skyscrapers that would have given the French capital a New York-style skyline.

The 1905-11 Palais Stoclet in Brussels (*centre top*) was designed by Josef Hoffmann (and furnished by Hoffmann and other prominent designers of the Vienna Secession and Wiener Werkstätte). The fifty-room marble and bronze mansion exhibited some proto-Moderne features, including a stepped tower, ornamental metalwork and prominent statuary. Owner Adolf Stoclet was the uncle of French architect Robert Mallet-Stevens, who was much influenced by the house.

Secession-period structures of *fin-de-siècle* Vienna, with their balanced use of both rectilinear elements and decorative details, arguably comprise the most direct antecedents of Art Deco architecture. Much of the façade of Otto Wagner's 1904-6 Austrian Post Office Savings Bank (*above*) was clad in thin marble slabs bolted together. The openwork bronze dome of the glorious 1898 Secession building by Joseph Maria Olbrich (*below*) was originally (and is once again) gilded.

Eliel Saarinen's 1904-14 Railway Station in Helsinki (*above*) was a considerable influence on later monumental Art Deco structures (especially in the United States, where Saarinen settled in 1923); note the four figures sculpted by Emil Wikstrom flanking the main entrance, the deft massing of stone and the dominant tower.

The rigid rectilinearity of Frank Lloyd Wright's 1904 Larkin Administration Building in Buffalo (*opposite above left*) was softened by Richard W. Bock's terracotta ornament, which included stylized floral designs on the piers. This monumental brick office building (demolished in 1949-50) helped set the stage for many Art Deco-era workplaces.

More than any other British buildings – and much like those of the Viennese Secessionists – the creations of Scotsman Charles Rennie Mackintosh looked forward to aspects of Art Deco architecture; for instance, the ornamental metalwork, window grids and stepped segments seen in the west view of his 1898-1907 Glasgow School of Art (*opposite above right*).

A striking vertical form characterized Joseph Maria Olbrich's 1907 Hochzeitsturm (Wedding Tower) (*right*) in Darmstadt. The five-part stepped roof of the tower was apparently meant to signify a hand, but it uncannily foreshadows later New York skyscrapers.

Several significant early twentieth-century factories in eastern Europe, such as Peter Behrens' 1908-9 A.E.G. turbine factory in Berlin (*right*) and Hans Poelzig's 1912 chemical plant (*opposite below*) in Luban near Posen (now Poznań, Poland), had a strong bearing on later industrial architecture. No longer were such structures faceless masses of brick, glass and metal.

One of Russia's most significant architects in the nineteen-twenties and thirties was Konstantin Melnikov, whose 1927 Moscow house (*above*), its double-cylindrical form dotted with some sixty hexagonal windows, was a striking Modernist structure.

Among the immediate precursors and contemporaries of Art Deco architecture were some striking European designs, including the three domed structures on this page: Bruno Taut's Glass Pavilion at the Cologne Werkbund exhibition of 1914 (*top*); the 1917-21 Einstein Tower at Potsdam (*above left*) by Erich Mendelsohn; and Antonio Sant'Elia's 1912 design for Monza Cemetery (*left*).

The Scheepvaarthuis, Amsterdam (*above*) (by Johan van der Mey, with Piet Kramer and Michel de Klerk 1912-16) was one of the most influential Amsterdam School projects. The massive brick office building was noteworthy for its abundant use of stylized elements, a course that was later adopted by the creators of many American Art Deco skyscrapers.

Michel de Klerk's domestic projects combined the decorative and utilitarian in such a way as to result in handsome housing estates at the time unique in Europe. One such was the Eigen Haard (Own Hearth) housing association project, which included the 1917 building (*right*), notable for its textured brickwork, diverse windows and lively asymmetry.

31

Adolf Loos, the Austrian architect who equated ornament with crime in 1908, designed the Steiner House, Vienna (*opposite above left*) in 1910; it looked forward to later European structures such as Bernard Bijvoet and Johannes Duiker's 1925 Aalsmeer house (*opposite above right*) and Robert Mallet-Stevens' Cubist private houses of 1926-27 in Paris (*opposite below*).

Two seminal modern buildings in Germany were designed by Walter Gropius: the Fagus Shoe Factory in Alfeld an der Leine (*below*), a 1910-11 collaborative effort with Adolf Meyer, and the 1926 Bauhaus building in Dessau (*right*).

The majority of newly built British and American private residences of the nineteen-twenties and thirties largely reflected a penchant for past architectural styles, with dwellings in the Modernist and Moderne (i.e. Art Deco) fashions far less common; the Highpoint One high-rise flats (*left*) in Highgate, London (Berthold Lubetkin and Tecton, 1933-35) were an innovative multi-storey structure for London, just as Frank Lloyd Wright's 1936 Kaufmann House (Fallingwater) (*below*) in Bear Run, Pennsylvania. was revolutionary, not only in its dramatic multi-cantilevered form, but also in its sympathetic relationship with a rural environment; a similar concern for setting was exhibited by Viennese-born, Wright-influenced Richard J. Neutra in his 1927-29 house for Dr Phillip Lovell (*below left*) on a Los Angeles hillside.

These three white-washed, rectilinear residences are examples of Modernism at its purest. E-1027 (*above*), Eileen Gray's cliff-dwelling Riviera residence of 1927, was designed for and in collaboration with publisher Jean Badovici. Wells Coates's elegant, balconied Lawn Road flats (*right*), in Hampstead, London (1933), made an early International Style statement; and Le Corbusier and Pierre Jeanneret's 1929-31 Villa Savoye (*below right*), in Poissy-sur-Seine, was a somewhat incongruous cube-on-*pilotis* in a verdant country setting.

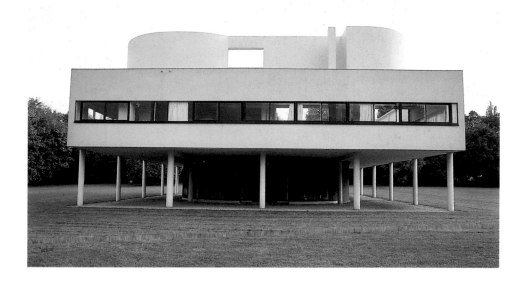

Chapter 3

International Expositions

As American industrial designer Walter Dorwin Teague simply and succinctly put it in his 1940 book, *Design This Day*: 'Because of its impermanence and legitimately bizarre character, exposition design has served as an experimental field for new structural forms and expressions'. Teague was in fact referring specifically to American fairs of the mid to late nineteen-thirties with their preponderance of Streamline Moderne pavilions, but the same words could more or less be applied to all the major international exhibitions of the twenties and thirties, including the 1925 Paris Exposition, the premier showcase of Art Deco. Not only did this fair – the word seems inadequate for such a spectacle of light, colour, design and good (and even some bad) taste – spotlight the achievements of contemporary design and industry, it limited itself to the present, even projecting a bit into the future, but officially forbidding any blatant historicizing, celebrating or replicating of the past. Its influential, much-publicized architecture mostly comprised structures that later came to be known as Art Deco, although some examples of Modernism and, notwithstanding the fair's ban, traditional styles were also represented.

1925 Paris Exposition

No preceding world fair was to have quite the impact of the Exposition Internationale des Arts Décoratifs et Industriels Modernes, which lasted from April to October 1925.

The Exposition occupied a huge area in the centre of Paris, and its overall organization was the work of its chief architect, Charles Plumet, and Louis Bonnier, who was in charge of landscaping. The fair's main gate, the Porte d'Honneur, next to the Grand Palais, led one through the fair across the Seine, via the Pont Alexandre III and down the long Esplanade to the Place des Invalides. Along the route, including sites on the bridge and at moorings in the Seine, were over 130 individual showplaces of artistic, commercial and industrial establishments, with hundreds more individual artists, manufacturers and commercial establishments displaying their wares in the massive Grand Palais. Over twenty nations participated – not, however, Germany (which had not been invited) and the United States (which declined the invitation) – though a few did not build entire pavilions for their displays. To the west, even the Eiffel Tower was dressed up at night for the spectacle, its frame clad in a Moderne illuminated display sponsored by Citroën (whose logo appeared on one of the nine changing patterns comprising the six-coloured light show).

Opposite

Hall of Science, A Century of Progress exhibition, Chicago, 1933-34.

In terms of being an influence on later design and architecture, the 1925 fair is unsurpassed in this century as a single event. Although celebrating a Gallic style which had by then reached its peak in France, thanks to the various specialist and general magazines which covered it, the fair served as a superb, all-encompassing, but sadly temporary introduction-cum-review to architects, designers and members of the public the world over. Its ephemeral nature notwithstanding, the bulk of the major pavilions were constructed of reinforced concrete over wooden frames, with a multitude of glass (clear and stained, decorative and functional), plaster and wrought-iron components, notably by Edgar Brandt, as well as the occasional modern material, such as plastic.

The most significant Art Deco structures were, not surprisingly, French in design (as discussed earlier, the building which was to have the most far-reaching effect of all those in the fair was Le Corbusier's L'Esprit Nouveau, which was decidedly not Art Deco). These included the pavilions of the Parisian department stores, Galeries Lafayette, Le Bon Marché, Louvre and Le Printemps; those of *ensembliers* Ruhlmann and Süe et Mare; the two pavilions of Sèvres; and Robert Mallet-Stevens' Pavillon du Tourisme. Other domestic pavilions of note were those of the French diamond and precious-stone dealers, book publishers Crès & Cie, glassmaker René Lalique and Christofle-Baccarat.

The three principal gateways (out of thirteen) were the Porte d'Honneur, the Porte d'Orsay and the Porte de la Concorde, all stunning, towering achievements. Pierre Patout's ten massive square columns at the Place de la Concorde encircled a bank of trees and Louis Dejean's welcoming statue of an open-armed, gilt-bronzed woman set on a socle with bas-relief carving by the Martel twins, Jan and Joël. The Porte d'Orsay entrance was designed by Louis Boileau and comprised a huge blue and gold nameplate-banner on a densely patterned Art Deco ground at the front, an allegorical fresco by Louis Voguet, depicting 'l'Art Décoratif', on the back. The sides of the high gate were fashioned as stylized scrolling fountains, a leitmotif of the fair. Indeed, the bubbling fountain was the theme of the main entrance at the Porte d'Honneur, by Henri Favier and André Ventre, with sculpture by Henri Navarre and glass by Lalique. Four pairs of columns, each column surmounted by a stylized fountain, each pair connected by a figurative frieze over the pedestrian gate, flanked the roadway, and the pairs were stepped back and conjoined to the next gate by ironwork grilles by Edgar Brandt, again with a fountain motif.

Beginning with Primavera, established by Printemps in 1913, the four above-named Parisian department stores had set up design ateliers in the dozen years preceding the Exposition. The pavilions were arresting, extravagant and, above all, inviting – their *raison d'être*, after all, was to get the visitors through their doors to see the room settings, artworks and other objects that were on view. The Primavera pavilion, designed by Sauvage & Vybo, was the most striking of all, though less for its decoration than its simple mushroom shape. Its ceramic-clad mound of a roof was encrusted with Lalique glass bosses, its doorway flanked by two massive pillars. Its most prominent decoration, in fact, was organic but not stylized: real plants sat atop the pillars and all along both the bottom of the dome and the ground. The Studium-Louvre pavilion was an octagon surmounted by a smaller octagon, and it, too, featured a plethora of live plants. There was also a great deal of conventionalized ornament, including an octet of carved stone urns overflowing with stylized blossoms at the upper levels, these by Albert Laprade, who also designed the pavilion. Metalwork by the ubiquitous *ferronnier*, Edgar Brandt, provided additional features.

Galeries Lafayette's white marble-clad La Maîtrise pavilion (designed by Joseph Hiriart, Georges Tribout and Georges Beau) was the most dramatic of the four: above the doorway was a huge leaded-glass and gilt-bronze window by Jacques Gruber depicting a colourful sunburst, and topping four huge grooved columns aside the entrance were four allegorical sculptures by Léon Leyritz, symbolizing feather, fur, lace and ribbon. Le Bon Marché's Pomone pavilion, like La Maîtrise's 'temple', consisted of stepped segments. Designed by Louis Boileau, it, too, featured a massive overdoor decoration of leaded glass, in this case with a geometric pattern of semicircles, zigzags and circles. Most unusual about this pavilion was that practically every segment of its exterior featured a pattern, usually of zigzag lines: there was even such a motif on the front of the stairs leading up to the entrance. These four buildings, of course, could never have been built in a setting other than a temporary one. But they were meant to be attention-getters and crowd-pleasers, and for that they served the purpose.

Far more sedate and aesthetically pleasing were the two 'concept' pavilions of *ensembliers* Ruhlmann and Süe et Mare. The Groupe Ruhlmann's 'L'Hôtel du Collectionneur' was overseen by Jacques-Emile Ruhlmann and featured within the works of the finest designers of the day, and Louis Süe and André Mare's La Compagnie des Arts Français created the 'Musée d'Art Contemporain'. The latter featured a simple dome atop a Louis-Seize-inspired, square building, with only a few bas-reliefs for decoration. Ruhlmann's pavilion, which was apparently the most admired at the fair (admittedly for its contents not its package), was essentially a square, stepped building with a bay at the back. It was designed by Pierre Patout and embellished with a gate by Edgar Brandt and, above the front door and on a frieze along the upper bay at the rear, classical bas-reliefs of dancers by Joseph Bernard. Indeed, there appeared even more noble figures outside the pavilion: on frescoes by Henri Marret, and in a figural group at the back by Alfred-Auguste Janniot, entitled 'Hommage à la gloire de Jean Goujon' (the French Renaissance sculptor).

The Pavillons de Sèvres were remarkable not only for the two tasteful ceramic-sheathed buildings by Pierre Patout and André Ventre, but also for the lovely garden that divided them, with a *grès* fountain in the middle by Henri Bouchard, colourful stone and terrazzo mosaic tiling on the ground, and handsome porcelain and *grès* statuary all around. Towering over the manufactory's display were six monumental ceramic-clad urns surmounted by fountain-like forms and decorated on most of their surfaces with a pattern of stylized blossoms.

Robert Mallet-Stevens' Pavillon du Tourisme, much like his largely domestic projects in France, veered more towards Modernism and might even have been mistaken for a serious De Stijl structure. Yet something about its nature – basically it was a rectangular building dominated by a giant Modernist clock tower – saved it from utter severity.

Among the other French pavilions, that of the diamond and precious-stone dealers was an utterly fantastic domed structure faceted at the top, like a diamond, with Y-shaped segments holding up the dome – the setting – decorated with a pattern of scrolls, circles and triangles. The architects were Jacques Lambert, Gus Saacke and Pierre Bailly, who were no doubt partly inspired by Bruno Taut's Glass Pavilion at the 1914 Deutscher Werkbund exhibition in Cologne, with its crystalline faceted cupola. More playfully symbolic was the Crès & Cie pavilion, designed by Hiriart, Tribout and Beau, its front conceived as three partially open books on end, their zigzag-patterned upper spines jutting outwards.

The Lalique and Christofle-Baccarat pavilions struck more serious notes. The latter, by Baccarat chief Georges Chevalier, was a square topped by a small fluted dome and featuring two huge square pillars alongside the double-door entrance. Bas-reliefs on the sides showed glass and metal craftsmen at work. René Lalique designed his own pavilion (Marc Ducluzeaud was the architect who realized it), the simplest of cubes with a cubic extension on either side. The severity of form was lightened by its decoration, however: the huge four-part steel door with glass by Lalique decorated with flowers (it was executed by L. Maison), and Sèvres ceramic panels, also with floral designs, skirted the cornice. Nearby was a huge obelisk fountain of Lalique's design, formed of sixteen tiers of 128 moulded-glass caryatids of different miens, most allegorical figures relating to water.

Located on both sides of the Pont Alexandre III – which had been built for the 1900 Exposition – was a garland of forty coloured-plaster boutiques, of which Maurice Dufrêne was the overall designer. The shops featured, among other items, Sonia Delaunay fashions and accessories, Lalique glass, Pleyel pianos (including one by Ruhlmann), Revillon furs, Tétard silver, Paul Kiss metalwork, even the dental products of Dentifrices Bi-oxyne. These storefronts, like others in the fair and many in Paris proper, featured various motifs from the Art Deco repertoire – distinctive Moderne lettering, stylized blossoms, classical figures, geometric patterns – etched into glass, moulded out of plaster or painted on to signs.

Many of the foreign pavilions were undistinguished reworkings of traditional designs, some with perhaps slight concessions to modern design appearing somewhere on their façades. But some made very strong Moderne statements, reflecting movements within their countries or translating period and vernacular styles into a contemporary language. The U.S.S.R. pavilion, by Konstantin Melnikov, was a brazen, mostly glass and wood Constructivist structure, with white and red painted sections. Danish

Paris's present-day Musée des Arts Africains et Océaniens, designed by Albert Laprade, originated as the Musée des Colonies at the 1931 Exposition Internationale Coloniale. The façade of the Neoclassical pile is covered with a massive bas-relief frieze depicting life and work in various French colonies; it was created by Art Deco sculptor Alfred-Auguste Janniot and executed by some thirty carvers over a three-year period.

and Dutch pavilions were in a more natural red brick. Both of them were executed in relatively restrained traditional-national styles (the former was by Kay Fisker, the latter by J.F. Staal). On the other hand, Joseph Czajkowski's Polish Pavilion updated a provincial style: the three-tiered, steeple-like tower sitting on top of a cubic base was a lively essay in geometric shapes, enlivened by the steeple's organic finials. Victor Horta, the Belgian architect so closely identified with the curvilinear Art Nouveau style, designed a sombre, stepped, rectilinear pavilion for his country, its highlights figural bas-reliefs by Pierre Braecke and allegorical statues by Marcel Wolfers representing 'l'Art Décoratif'.

After the 1925 Fair

The years following the 1925 Paris Exposition saw its ideas and output borrowed, distilled and adapted for various other markets. The likes of its exuberant Art Deco pavilions would not be seen again in a temporary exhibition, but traces would resurface here and there – at the Hispanic-American Exposition at Seville in 1929, the Exposition Internationale at Liège in 1930 (where the Palace of Electricity, with its ziggurat façade, stood out) and the fair in Stockholm the same year.

There was yet another fair in Paris in 1931, the Exposition Internationale Coloniale, which celebrated the achievements of the French in various colonies, as well as at home, but included the participation of Belgium, Denmark, Portugal, Brazil, the United States and other countries. Native-style pavilions, among them a reconstruction of the temple at Angkor Wat, dominated the fair, along with the Musée des Colonies, a massive Neoclassical stone box set within a peristyle and designed by Albert Laprade. The façade of the museum comprised a massive bas-relief frieze by the Art Deco sculptor Alfred-Auguste Janniot; it took thirty craftsmen three years to carve the various figures and vignettes depicting life and work in French colonial Africa, Polynesia and other locales.

A Century of Progress, Chicago, 1933-34

Although fairs continued to be held in Europe through the nineteen-thirties, much attention was now focused on the monumental exhibitions being mounted in the United States. The most important, certainly in architectural if not other terms, was the 1933-34 Century of Progress Exposition in Chicago, which marked the centenary of the founding of the Midwestern city and featured as its theme 'Science in Industry'. A financial as well as artistic success, some thirty-eight million people visited the fair over its seventeen-month duration (it ran a year over its originally intended length) – and this despite the recent Depression.

One of the stars of the fair was the Travel and Transportation Building (Edward H. Bennett, Hubert Burnham and John A. Holabird), a giant engineering as well as design feat: using a suspension-bridge type construction, its roof was made up of metal plates suspended by steel support cables from a dozen steel towers grounded in concrete slabs, eliminating the need for any columns or other impedimenta within the exhibition space. Its windowless (in common with most of the pavilions) exterior was dominated by giant sunburst motifs, reminiscent of the La Maîtrise pavilion at the Paris 1925 fair. But whereas Jacques Gruber's ornate orb was of gilt-bronze and coloured glass, the less exuberant, yet nobler Chicago suns were of monochromatic metal. Also outstanding was the Administration Building, by the same trio of Chicago architects, a massive rectangular building featuring a huge allegorical figure on either side. Indeed, allegorical bas-relief sculptures and paintings abounded at the fair, representing such forces as atomic energy, electricity and light (more 'representative' was the Havoline Thermometer Building, by Alfonso Iannelli, in the shape of a giant stepped thermometer). The sculptor Leo Friedlander created four huge Streamline Moderne gypsum pylons with figures at the bottom symbolizing the four basic elements; these were at the entrance to the Hall of Science pavilion, which was designed by Raymond M. Hood. In front of the Electrical Building (also by Hood) were the two pylons comprising sculptor Lee Lawrie's Water Gate, the bas-reliefs on one representing atomic energy, on the other stellar energy.

An integral element of the Chicago fair was its colours. The arrangement of the buildings may have been somewhat scattered and unpremeditated, but its palette was well thought out. Indeed, Joseph Urban, the Austrian-born architect, was entrusted with the fair's colour coordination, and he employed 23 shades in an effort to harmonize the 424-acre area. Each structure contained three to four colours (the Administration Building's were white, grey, and light and dark blue, with red trim), and surrounding elements – flagstaffs, kiosks and lamp-posts – were rendered in complementary shades. If the look by day was striking, the nocturnal effect was dazzling, since Urban employed state-of-the-art lighting (including, for the first time, neon tubing) to enhance the pavilions.

Chicago's aesthetic message proclaiming the union of science and industry was heard – and in many cases repeated – by other fair organizers in the nineteen-thirties. Though not worldwide in scope, the 1936 Texas Centennial Exposition in Dallas included pavilions (many of which still stand) of the monumental Moderne type that defined Chicago 1933-34 (the architecture was called 'Classic-Modern'), and indeed some of the same architects worked at both fairs. Massive allegorical figures adorned long, sometimes multi-cubed, low structures highlighted with colour, such as the Livestock Building (designed by the fair's coordinator, Dallas architect George L. Dahl), which was punctuated with zigzag patterns.

The Frontier Centennial Exposition, held in nearby Fort Worth at the same time, featured a variety of Western, Mayan and Native American subjects in the Moderne mode on its three principal structures, the Will Rogers Memorial Auditorium, Coliseum and Tower. These included stylized scrolls, wings and blossoms, stepped and geometric segments, rodeo riders and, on polychromed tile mosaic friezes along the entablatures, the sagas of the founding and industrial development of the West (on the auditorium) and of the men and women of the Southwest (on the coliseum).

The 1938 Empire Exhibition in Glasgow was a huge success; despite trying weather conditions, it was attended by over thirteen million people. This postcard detail amusingly contrasts Thomas Tait's starkly Moderne all-metal Tower of Empire with a quaint country village.

Other Fairs of the Nineteen-Thirties

Several major expositions took place in Europe in the mid to late nineteen-thirties, including Brussels (1935), yet again Paris (1937) and Glasgow (1938). On the whole, these three fairs broke no new ground in architecture or design.

The two dominant pavilions of the Paris exhibition were the facing monumental stone towers of Germany and the U.S.S.R.. The former was surmounted by a golden eagle, holding between its talons a wreath encircling a swastika, and the latter − a stepped structure − topped by a huge statue of a young man and woman wielding a hammer and sickle.

One display harked back nostalgically to 1925, the Pavillon du Tourisme designed by P. Sardou as a rectilinear tower emerging from an L-shaped structure with curving sides, all in shades of peach and cream. The tower made an obvious reference to Robert Mallet-Stevens' Tourism Pavilion a dozen years earlier (as did in fact Thomas Tait's all-metal Tower of Empire at the 1938 Empire Exhibition in Glasgow). The Musée d'Art Moderne and facing Palais de Chaillot at Trocadéro, both extant, were striking colonnaded rectilinear piles whose apparent severity was mitigated by the wealth of classical bas-reliefs on their façades and statuary around their perimeters.

The final pre-war exhibitions in the United States were the 1939 Golden Gate International Exposition in San Francisco and the 1939-40 New York World Fair.

The West Coast fair, which opened on 12 February and closed on 2 December 1939, was entirely purpose-built on 'Treasure Island', lagoon-dotted land that had been reclaimed from the bay. Its *raison d'être* was to celebrate the area and, more importantly, the openings of the Golden Gate Bridge and the San Francisco-Oakland Bay Bridge, 'the world's greatest spans of steel', as a Treasure Island brochure boasted. Twenty-eight foreign countries took part in the fair, along with fifteen states and numerous commercial establishments and regional organizations.

The fair's planning committee comprised, among others, Timothy L. Pflueger, an important West Coast architect whose projects made use of both Art Deco and Modernist elements, with a fair sprinkling of Mayan Revival and Neoclassical thrown in. Its major pavilions, flanking the Courts of the Moon, Pacifica, Seven Seas, Flowers and Reflections, were mostly elaborate stepped structures, decorated with and set amid stylish sculptures and murals by West Coast artists. The smaller South and Central American displays were tasteful, up-to-date interpretations of traditional forms, including the Mayan-inspired Guatemala Pavilion, the Peru Pavilion, modelled after an Incan temple, and Ecuador's pylon-like display, with a huge sun over the door and geometric designs along the top and bottom. As at the Chicago fair six years earlier, light and colour were important aspects of the Golden Gate Exposition, only this time the structures were generally white and the colour was provided at night by the huge array of multi-hued lights (for example, the principal colour of the Court of the

Seven Seas was apricot). The buildings were far more ordered, the entire display far more pleasing and symmetrical than at Chicago, however, especially the areas comprising the principal attractions.

The New York World Fair, occupying some 1,216 acres in Flushing, Queens, was an ambitious, unrealistically optimistic (considering the impending war) undertaking, with a host of significant architects and industrial designers taking part, including Alvar Aalto, Norman Bel Geddes, Henry Dreyfuss, Raymond Loewy, Gilbert Rohde, Walter Dorwin Teague, Ely Jacques Kahn, Harrison & Fouilhoux, Shreve, Lamb & Harmon, Skidmore & Owings and Voorhees, Walker, Foley & Smith. Its first season extended from 30 April to 31 October 1939, and in 1940 (by which time the U.S.S.R. pavilion had been demolished and a few other nations were also not participating) the fair was open from 11 May to 27 October. Interestingly, the contents and purposes of some buildings changed from 1939 to 1940; here we discuss them as they were originally in 1939.

The World of Tomorrow's 'Theme Center', located in the middle of the main exhibition area, comprised a simple obelisk and sphere of monumental proportions loftily named the Trylon (from triangular pylon) and Perisphere. The pair, designed by the firm of Wallace K. Harrison and J. André Fouilhoux, were painted pure white and together surpassed all that was around them, both in height (the Trylon's was 700 feet) and width (the Perisphere's was 200 feet).

The Board of Design of the fair issued fairly flexible guidelines on pavilions to the participants, which numbered sixty foreign exhibitors in addition to thirty-three states and territories and innumerable private companies. The buildings were to be fairly low (except for the Trylon), creative but not shocking (as many of those at Chicago were deemed to be), and neither historic replicas nor traditional structures (except in the American States section). Since pavilions were air-conditioned, windows were few, making painted murals and sculpted reliefs on exteriors plentiful. The colour guidelines for the principal areas were perhaps the most detailed, though they were not always strictly adhered to, and discreet, subtle exceptions could be made: those buildings directly around the Theme Center were to be off-white, while those along the main axis, Constitution Mall, were to be rendered in shades of red, which darkened with increasing distance from the Theme Center. The Avenue of Patriots, north of the Center, was to have yellow and gold pavilions, the easterly Avenue of Pioneers shades of blue. Joining the termini of these three main arteries was Rainbow Avenue, along which were structures of varied hues.

Several of the major pavilions were noteworthy for their Moderne aspects. The Ford Motor Company display (Albert Kahn, Inc.; Walter Dorwin Teague, designer) was a sprawling complex of curves, cylinders and arcs, its entryway dominated by Robert Foster's arresting free-standing sculpture of Mercury hovering above the doors. That quintessential thirties exhibition structure, the massive free-standing or attached pylon, was much in evidence in New York: a blue one clung like a giant handle to the

Electrical Products Building (A. Stewart Walker and Leon N. Gillette), which itself resembled a mammoth iron, and the arresting quartet of 65-foot-high stepped pylons symbolizing the four basic elements, with four dozen relief sculptures by Carl Paul Jennewein, were both sculpture and architecture.

The exhibition had its fair share of symbolic structures: the radio tube-shaped Radio Corporation of America (RCA) Building (Skidmore & Owings); the Marine Transportation Building's two huge super-liner prows (Ely Jacques Kahn and Muschenheim & Brounn); the Singing Tower of Light, representing electric power, in the Westinghouse pavilion forecourt; the glass powder box-like top of the Coty Inc. pavilion; the stainless-steel zigzag lightning bolt capping the General Electric Company Building (Voorhees, Walker, Foley & Smith), symbolizing the taming of the savage forces of electricity; and the fluted Star Pylon (Francis Keally and Leonard Dean), representing electricity's force. There were massive advertising gimmicks as well, such as Walter Dorwin Teague's forty-foot-high till atop the cylindrical National Cash Register Company pavilion, regularly totting up the number of fair attendees.

New materials, or new uses for old materials, appeared, perhaps no more wittily than on the American Radiator & Standard Sanitary Corporation Building (Voorhees, Walker, Foley & Smith): this sprawling arc, orange-yellow in colour and on the Avenue of Patriots, was fronted by a row of Ionic columns made up of standard three-foot sections of flue lining, with coiled copper-pipe volutes. Furthering this large-scale artifice/analogy, valves, radiators and pipe fittings made up the grillework on the building.

Some of the liveliest, most ornate structures were situated in the Food Zone, where Moderne elements of both the Streamline and French-inspired varieties played parts in starring and subsidiary roles. The circular Schaefer Center (Eggers & Higgins), a restaurant-bar complex, was topped with a stylized fountain motif straight out of the 1925 Paris Exposition, and the Sealtest Building (De Witt Clinton Pond), shaped like three-quarters of a round of cheese, was surmounted by three massive winged forms, like those on the Empire State Building's spire. The American Tobacco Company pavilion (Francisco & Jacobus), with its fluted semicircular segments, resembled a sedate Deco cinema and, but for the stylized cow heads alternating with the words 'Borden' on its crown, the cylindrical Borden Company Building (Voorhees, Walker, Foley & Smith), encircled by two Saturn-like rings at the top, was reminiscent of one of Charles Holden's early nineteen-thirties London Underground stations.

The fair's largest, most spectacular display, and the one most firmly rejecting the past, was General Motors' Highways and Horizons exhibition, designed by Norman Bel Geddes (Albert Kahn, Inc., architects). It was conceived as a nineteen-sixties-era complex made up of a quartet of interconnected structures. Walter Dorwin Teague called them 'finely rhythmical in a fresh vernacular', and these architectural elements duly rejected not only the past, but even the late-Moderne present, with their futuristic forms and lack of decoration.

International Expositions

The 1925 Exposition Internationale des Arts Décoratifs et Industriels Modernes in Paris – from which the term 'Art Deco' was derived – was the apogee of *le style moderne* in France. Though its domestic and foreign pavilions were fugitive structures – albeit mostly of reinforced concrete – razed at the fair's conclusion, many of their decorative aspects lived on in future, permanent buildings.

The three pavilions illustrated here made ample use of stock Art Deco motifs: stylized blossoms, scrolls, stepped forms, zigzags and other geometric patterns: the Pomone atelier pavilion of Le Bon Marché, the department store, by Louis Boileau (*above*); the City of Paris building (R. Bouvard, A. Vincent, Six & Labrenille) (*left above*); and Galeries Lafayette's La Maîtrise pavilion (Hiriart, Tribout & Beau), with its sunburst of gilt-bronze and coloured glass by Jacques Gruber (*left*).

J.F. Staal's Dutch Pavilion (*above*) featured textured brick as well as figural and other sculpted elements, all of which characterized much Dutch Expressionist architecture of the time. Another foreign display (*below*) was that of French Africa, whose architect, Germain Olivier, took native forms, flora and fauna and adapted them in a Moderne manner.

The output of the Primavera atelier of the *grand magasin*, Le Printemps, featured in Sauvage & Vybo's pyramidal pavilion (*top*), whose exterior was sheathed in ceramic inset with glass bosses fashioned by René Lalique.

The L'Hôtel du Collectionneur pavilion (*above*), presented by the Groupe Ruhlmann, was created by Pierre Patout. Its façade featured a frieze of dancers by Joseph Bernard, and in front was Alfred-Auguste Janniot's sculptural group, 'A la gloire de Jean Goujon'.

A Century of Progress, the international exposition that opened in 1933 in Chicago, marked the centenary of the founding of the Midwestern city and had as its theme 'Science in Industry'. Its massive pavilions combined Neoclassical and Streamline Moderne elements. One side of the circular court of Raymond M. Hood's Electrical Building (*left*) featured a sculptural mural of Energy, and two monumental figures flanked Bennett, Burnham & Holabird's Administration Building (*opposite above*). One of the fair's highlights was the same three architects' Travel and Transportation Building (*opposite below*), a superb engineering and design feat. Employing a suspension-bridge type construction, its roof comprised metal plates suspended by steel cables from a dozen steel towers grounded by concrete slabs, thus eliminating the need for any columns or other obstacles to the interior display space. Note the giant sunburst motifs over the entrance.

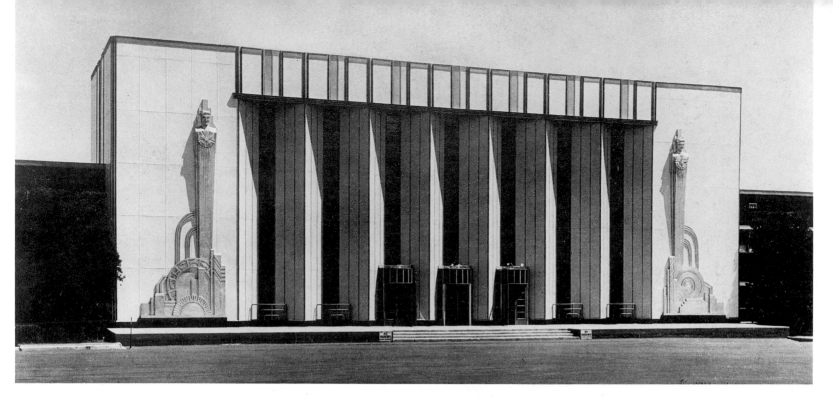

International expositions throughout Europe and North America proliferated in the nineteen-thirties. Their pavilions, ancillary arcades and fun fairs received millions of visitors, who sent postcards (usually black-and-white images hand-tinted with garish hues and then mass-manufactured) by the thousands to family and friends. Three such images appear on this page: the Palace of Mines at the 1930 Liège International Exposition (*left*); the Palace of Electricity at the same Belgian fair (*left centre*); and the Court of the Moon at the 1939 Golden Gate International Exposition, San Francisco (*left below*), the allegorical figure atop the Fountain of Phantom Arches representing the Evening Star.

The aim of the 1937 Paris Exposition Internationale des Arts et des Techniques Appliqués à la Vie Moderne was to show the compatibility of beauty and utility. The two dominant pavilions were the overtly political facing monumental stone towers of the U.S.S.R. and of Germany (*opposite above left*), designed by Albert Speer (with French architects Courrèges, Coudert, Jankowski & Hugonenq). Another turreted structure, the Pavillon du Tourisme designed by P. Sardou (*opposite above right*), paid homage to Robert Mallet-Stevens' Tourism Pavilion at the 1925 Paris Exposition. The white-washed severity of the fair's Musée d'Art Moderne (*opposite below*) was mitigated by the wealth of classical bas-reliefs on its façade and statuary around it; its architects were J.C. Dondel, A. Aubert, P. Viard & D. Dastugue.

The entrance to the 1937 Great Lakes Exposition in Cleveland was marked by seven 'towers of illumination' (*opposite above*) – huge, dazzling pylons meant to represent architectonic flaming candles. A far more sober pavilion was the Varied Industries, Electrical and Communications Building (*opposite below*) of the 1936 Texas Centennial held in Dallas. The 1939 Golden Gate Exposition in San Francisco was especially notable for allegorical statuary and fantasy architecture, such as the Moon and Dawn in front of the stepped Tower of the South and steepled Tower of the Moon (*below*) and the Elephant Towers of the fair's main entrance (*right*).

The 1939-40 World Fair in New York, 'Building the World of Tomorrow', was an ambitious, optimistic undertaking, with many noted architects and industrial designers participating. The fair's 'Theme Center' comprised a monumental obelisk and sphere – loftily named the Trylon (from triangular pylon) and Perisphere (*left*) – designed by the architects Harrison & Foulhoux. The two structures were depicted on a host of cheap souvenirs that could be bought at the exhibition, from plastic salt and pepper shakers (*below left*) to a drinking glass (*below*).

Some of the liveliest structures of the New York World Fair were situated in the Food Zone. The stylized-fountain motifs topping the Schaefer Center (*right below*) by Eggers & Higgin, a restaurant-bar complex, came out of the 1925 Paris Exposition, and the circular façade of Food Building No. 2 (*right above*), by Del Gaudio, Aspinwall & Simpson, was covered with a red and white mural by Pierre Bourdelle that depicted the 'housing of products destined to human consumption'. An architectural rendering of its theme, Shreve, Lamb & Harmon's Glass Center Building (*right centre*) was fashioned almost entirely out of glass.

Chapter 4

Residences and Hotels

Art Deco architecture was primarily concerned with public rather than private buildings, but there were nevertheless countless domestic examples of the style in a number of countries, from modest dwellings to high-rise hotels and apartment complexes.

Private Houses

Much like its Modernist counterpart, the Art Deco domestic dwelling was not especially popular in the nineteen-twenties and thirties. Most American homeowners, for instance, preferred a more traditional neo-Tudor or neo-Colonial residence, as can be discerned from scanning architectural or home-builder journals of the time. Indeed, the Art Deco style was mainly an unorthodox, even somewhat eccentric and elitist, choice for a home, although modestly priced examples were available.

The six houses in Auteuil, Paris, designed by Robert Mallet-Stevens (1886-1945) in 1926-27 and occupying the small street bearing his surname, comprise perhaps the finest complex of French Art Deco dwellings. The white-washed structures are basically Cubist in conception, but they are enlivened with curves, colour and decorative elements, such as leaded-glass windows with geometric patterns. Several early nineteen-twenties drawings by Mallet-Stevens depict handsome large-scale villas and country houses with decorated components, these showing more clearly than the Auteuil houses Mallet-Stevens' admiration for the Vienna Secession and Charles Rennie Mackintosh. Also in Paris, architect-designer Pierre Chareau (1883-1950) collaborated with Dutch architect Bernard Bijvoet on the 'Maison de Verre' (1928-31) for Dr Jean Dalsace. This three-storey house of revolutionary design – its façade comprising a wall of glass tiles with concave lenses (to allow internal lighting via external projectors), all set in a gridwork of iron – became something of a sensation and a rallying point for Modernists. A somewhat similar glazing material, the glass brick or block, became closely identified with more populist examples of Art Deco architecture, especially in the United States.

Most Parisian dwellings with Art Deco decoration were multi-storey apartment buildings. In the street called the Villa Seurat, however, where Salvador Dali, Chaïm Soutine and André Lurçat once lived, are several Modernist designs as well as an Auguste Perret building with an interesting patterned façade. Art Deco decoration was added to domestic structures throughout France, especially in the south. The buildings themselves were

Opposite

Entrance to a Streamline Moderne Los Angeles apartment building by Milton J. Black, *c.*1938.

Kem Weber's *c.*1930 house for Dr and Mrs J.C. Friedman (*left*) in Banning, California, featured vividly painted beams on its white-brick exterior; an anonymously designed *c.*1940 house in Dyersburg, Tennessee (*above left*), included porthole windows, cantilevered 'eyebrow' over the door and glass bricks; and a modest early thirties residence (*above*) in the Napier, New Zealand, suburb of Marewa contained stepped arches.

Among Frank Lloyd Wright's private houses were four concrete textile-block California structures of Mayan inspiration, including the 1923 Los Angeles residence of Dr John Storer (*opposite*). It was built of plain and patterned pre-cast concrete blocks 'woven' together with horizontal and vertical 'threads' of reinforced steel; the Storer House was painstakingly restored in the nineteen-eighties under architects Eric Lloyd Wright (Frank's grandson) and Martin Eli Weil.

mostly undistinguished (either Modernist or traditional) forms, but this did enable the decoration, such as floral panels and ornate grillework, to stand out. Also, in parts of French-colonized North Africa, Moderne villas were an alternative for the wealthy, as we can see from a period advertisement for Le Foyer Nord-Africain in Algiers offering handsome Art Deco-style and Modernist homes in Oran, Sfax, Tunis and Algiers.

The Bauhaus/International Style influence – as well as that of traditional vernacular styles – predominated in domestic architecture in Continental Europe. There were curved bays, plentiful windows (square, porthole and rectangular) and stepped segments on mostly white-washed, square-segment cottages and villas in Austria, Germany, Hungary, Czechoslovakia, Italy, Poland and Switzerland, though such elements alone certainly did not make a house Art Deco. Still, such dwellings were far from cold, calculated, purely rectilinear edifices. Examples include Heinrich Lauterbach's Hasek House in Gablonz, Germany, Lois Welzenbacher's Rosenbauer House in Austria, Adolph Rading's Haeffuer House in Pichelsdorf (1928), Alberto Sartoris's artisan's house at Turin (c.1930), Farkas Molnár's c.1933 house on a Budapest hillside and J.K. Riha's 1931 Riha House in Prague.

In Britain, Modernist homes were far more common than those of the Art Deco genre, although a good many white, rectilinear dwellings can be considered Art Deco by virtue of their curved balconies, stepped sections, metalwork details and added colour. White-washed, curved-sided homes – some with porthole windows – dotted many British seaside towns, such as William Walter Wood's 'White Walls', Torquay (1932), and the dozen or so 1934-35 designs at Frinton-on-Sea, Essex, by Oliver Hill (1887-1962). Hill's projects included both the traditional and contemporary, but he was influenced by the 1925 Paris Exposition, as the subtle, Moderne-tinged elegance of some commissions shows. Foremost among these was 'Joldwyns' (1930–33), in Holmbury St. Mary, Surrey, a complex of round and cubed white shapes, its front door flanked by metal sculptures of two sleek Art Deco does. Other British houses with Art Deco Moderne touches include German architect Peter Behrens' 'New Ways' (1926), W.J. Bassett-Lowke's Northampton residence; Thomas S. Tait's home in Newbury, Berkshire (c.1929), a modified ziggurat with emerald-green details; and P.D. Hepworth's rectilinear house in Kent (c.1931), its white surface brightened by orange and red shutters with a zigzag motif, yellow window frames and jade green tile copings.

Elsewhere in Britain, a small number of Modernist homes, some with Art Deco decoration, were built in the nineteen-thirties; these were generally white, flat-roofed, Cubist structures, with big windows, terraces, metal railings and, as on 'Geragh' (1937-38), Michael Scott's handsome house in Sandycove, County Dublin, curved bays. A generic Streamline Moderne home, designed in 1935 by William A. Gladstone, was built in Mansewood, Glasgow; it bore an uncanny resemblance to the 1935-36 E.E. Butler House in Des Moines, Iowa (Kraetsch & Kraetsch), thus nicely illustrating the truly international aspect of this subcategory of Art Deco.

Thomas S. Tait, of the firm Sir John Burnet & Partners, designed this white cement-finished home in Newbury, Berkshire, c.1929. Of modified ziggurat form, it featured an emerald-green front door, balustrade and casements.

Art Deco houses of the Streamline Moderne variety appeared across the continental United States in the nineteen-thirties. There were also homes with Modernist bents featuring colour or some other added decoration and, on the West Coast, some showing Mayan or Aztec influence. Many made use of new materials, such as brushed aluminium and glass bricks.

In Midwestern Des Moines, the Streamline Moderne house built for Earl Butler (designed by the owner and George Kraetsch) was a dramatic split-level, poured-concrete structure. A chequerboard theme ran through the mid nineteen-thirties home of Mr and Mrs Lloyd H. Buhs of Detroit, which was designed by Hugh T. Keyes. Intended as an exemplar of Detroit-made materials and talent, the flat-roofed, white-washed, curved and streamlined structure was sponsored by the Detroit Board of Commerce.

Throughout the States, smart Moderne homes, mostly in concrete or stucco, were built, many in newly created suburbs. Simple Cubist shapes enhanced with coloured stripes characterized father and daughter Charles M. and Zoe Davis's one-bedroom mid nineteen-thirties 'Aparthomes' in Fort Worth, whose design was subsequently copied in several states. A unique home in that city was Fred W. Murphree's 1941 residence for the Martin E. Robin family, with its fluted pilasters, stepped sections and ornamental wrought-ironwork. Much grander were Charles M. Davis's own 1937 home, by Robert P. Woltz, and William D. Wenthoff's residence in Tulsa (1935), with its upper-level nautical vignette: a porthole window looking out on to a curved railing. Making a different travel analogy was the Richard Mandel House in Mount Kisco, New York (Edward Durell Stone, 1933-34), which one writer likened to 'a giant airplane' (actually, it had a Modernist bent, and resembled an aerodrome more than an aeroplane).

Decorative patterns in coloured and plain brickwork marked some Art Deco American homes, such as a residence in St. Paul Street, Baltimore, designed by John Ahlers in 1937. There was a ribbon moulding around the house's L-shape, but this was met at the corners by fluted verticals; in addition, a bold geometric pattern was created in several places with the white bricks. Also in Maryland were two quintessential Streamline Moderne houses, one with tan brick finish (in Hyattsville), the other stucco (in Camp Springs); both (and no doubt dozens more throughout America) were constructed following mail-order plans from the Garlinghouse Plan Service of Topeka, Kansas (these two date from 1948, but they could easily have been built a decade earlier).

California, especially the Los Angeles area, was rich in Art Deco homes, some built for Hollywood stars, for whom the style held much appeal. A Moderne home in Santa Monica was created c.1929 by MGM art director Cedric Gibbons (1893-1960) for himself and his actress wife, Dolores del Rio. The stucco-sheathed concrete structure, termed by a 1931 movie magazine as 'modernistic in the extreme', had a flat roof, narrow windows and black marble steps leading up to a polished metal door, which was framed by a rectangular arch of diminishing setback sections; the front gate was of polished rolled steel.

The Moderne villa appeared in many countries; Prince Asaka's 1933 Tokyo residence (*opposite above*) was created by architects of the Imperial Household Department for the prince, who had spent several years in France (its interior was largely designed by Parisian Henri Rapin). It now houses the Tokyo Metropolitan Teien Art Museum. In Sherbrooke, Victoria, Harry Norris designed the Streamline Moderne (or Modern Ship Style) Burnham Beeches (*opposite below left*) for Alfred Nicholas in 1933. On the other side of the world, 'Joldwyns' (*opposite below right*), in Holmbury St. Mary, Surrey, was created by Oliver Hill in 1934; the domestic complex, rebuilt from an old Philip Webb design, comprised both cylindrical and cubed shapes, several sun terraces and a tall semicircular window fronting a staircase.

In southern France, the Moderne villa was often embellished with floral panels and ornamental metalwork. Typical examples include a large house in Cimiez (*left*), in the hills above Nice, and another in Vaison-la-Romaine, Provence (*above*).

Though it could easily be mistaken for a private house, the vividly painted, racing-striped building (*right*) is in fact the Ed Lee Apartments, a Miami Beach multi-dwelling unit in 1321 Pennsylvania Avenue. It was designed by Henry Hohauser, one of the resort town's premier Art Deco architects, in 1936.

63

Streamline Moderne private and apartment houses were common sights in southern California in the thirties and forties. Frederick Monhoff designed the sleek, white-washed house (*left*) for Danish opera singer-actor Lauritz Melchior in 1940-41, while Milton J. Black created the two apartment buildings (*opposite*); both multi-dwelling units are a pleasing mix of straight- and curved-edge elements with striated decoration.

Following somewhat in his father's Mayan Revival footsteps was Lloyd Wright's 1926 concrete textile-block and stucco house for John Sowden (*above*). The gaping-jaw entrance of the quasi-pyramidal structure was surmounted by a huge window with a grid-frame. A comparatively large window dominated the far less severe front of 'New Ways' (*right*), a residence designed by German architect Peter Behrens in 1926 in Northampton, England.

The Rue Mallet-Stevens in Auteuil comprised six private villas designed by Robert Mallet-Stevens in 1926-27. The structures were essentially Cubist, but enhanced with coloured and curved elements. For example, the house-cum-studio (*above left*) of the twin sculptors, Jan and Joël Martel, featured red *pâte-de-verre* tiles sheathing the ceiling of the terrace on top of a cylindrical tower, which contained a red-highlighted leaded-glass window by Louis

Barillet. Next to the Martel home, Mme Reifenberg's villa (*opposite*) also included an elongated Barillet window, but this with a simple monochromatic palette.

Late in his career, French architect Henri Sauvage (1873-1932) planned several highly dramatic pyramidal structures that were never realized, including the housing projects (*above*) envisioned for the banks of the Seine.

The 1935-36 E.E. Butler House (*opposite above*) in Des Moines, Iowa, designed by owner Earl Butler and George Kraetsch of Kraetsch & Kraetsch, was one of the finest Streamline Moderne houses in North America. Its successful combination of straight lines and curves, stepped segments and decorative horizontal mouldings, as well as its setting on a gentle slope of land, made it an outstanding example of residential architecture of the time. No less handsome was this Moderne house (*opposite below*) on the Caribbean island of Puerto Rico.

Variations of the thirties Moderne house – a sleek, white-washed combination of curves and right angles – appeared in Europe and North America. The plain, utilitarian house (*above*) designed by Howe & Lescaze for Frederick N. Field is situated on the top of a Connecticut hill, while the locale of the comparatively simple and inexpensive home (*right*) by Farkas Molnár is a Budapest hillside.

In *c.*1931, London architect P.D. Hepworth designed a house in Kent (*below*) with glazed roof garden. Its creamy-white, angular form was enlivened by red and orange shutters with a zigzag motif; other polychrome touches included green tile copings and yellow window frames.

The pastel confections lining the residential streets of Miami Beach's Art Deco District make up the finest group of Moderne residences in the United States. The recently restored Marlin (*left*), 1200 Collins Avenue, was designed by L. Murray Dixon in 1939. The architect of the 1936 Delia Apartments, 1575 Michigan Avenue (*left below*), was M.J. Nadel. Both feature decorative plaques on their façades.

A mural by Alfred du Pont dominates Irving W. Goldstine and J.S. Malloch's San Francisco apartment house (*left centre*). The 1937 dwelling featured in the 1947 film *Dark Passage* (whose stars, Humphrey Bogart and Lauren Bacall, were once its residents).

The extended 'eyebrows' and streamlined curves of two Miami Beach buildings (*opposite left* and *below*) are painted in bright hues that counterpoint their lighter-coloured grounds; these jazzy new façades did not begin to appear with frequency until the nineteen-eighties, when designer Leonard Horowitz originated the Deco Revival pastel palette.

Manhattan 'Skyscraper Deco' structures include a great many high-rise apartment buildings as well as commercial structures. The New Amsterdam (*above*), designed by Margon & Holder in 1930, is located at West 86th Street and Amsterdam Avenue. Note its jazzy metal spandrels and the drape-like forms high up on its façade.

Georges Chiquet's striking bas-relief of agricultural workers adorned the façade of J. Hillard's 1934 Paris apartment building (*above*), in 16 Rue Chardon-Lagache, in the 16th *arrondissement*. Additional Moderne decoration included zigzag bands and other geometric motifs.

The 1932 Maison Barillet (*left*), located at 15 Square Vergennes in the 15th *arrondissement*, was another of architect Robert Mallet-Stevens' domestic projects in the French capital. Its elongated leaded-glass window was created by Louis Barillet, the artist-occupant who was also responsible for the decorated windows in the same architect's villas in the Rue Mallet-Stevens, Auteuil.

A common sight in North Africa in the twenties and thirties was the cubic and cylindrical white-washed high-rise apartment building, similar to those in France. This modern apartment house (*above left*) in Oran, Algeria, could have been transplanted from Paris. To the east, in the Cairo suburb of Gezira Island, this luxurious Streamline Moderne apartment house with nautical balconies (*above*) dates from the late nineteen-thirties; the extended caption on the 1937 photograph was entitled 'Oldest Country Shows Newest Architecture'.

Hotels in the Moderne style were built in many countries, and they ranged from simple structures with minimal decoration to ornate monoliths. The 430-room Hotel Martinez in Cannes (*above*), which first opened its seafront doors in 1929, has a façade studded with gilded-metal balconies and floral bas-reliefs. The white-washed concrete Masonic Hotel in Napier, New Zealand (*opposite above left*), was designed by W.J. Prouse in 1932 and features a handsome entrance: a striking pediment tops a suspended 'marquee' of leaded glass and metal spelling out the hotel's name.

Eric Gill's sea-horse sculptures stand guard high over the entrance tower of the Midland Hotel in Morecambe, designed by Oliver Hill in 1932-34 (*opposite left below*). The huge concave mass of the three-storey, white-painted, stucco-over-brick structure echoed the curve of the Lancashire shoreline it abutted.

In Glasgow's Sauchiehall Street, James W. Weddell's Streamline Moderne Beresford Hotel (*right*) was built by W. Beresford Inglis to accommodate visitors to the 1938 Empire Exhibition. Originally clad with black, red and mustard-yellow faience, the hotel was designed along cinematic lines – not surprising, since Inglis had designed several Glasgow movie houses. It is now Baird Hall, a residence of Strathclyde University.

Less luxuriant and ostentatious in design but no less tasteful were the homes of Berlin-born architect-designer Kem (for Karl Emanuel Martin) Weber (1889-1963). Weber designed film sets as well as buildings, as did Lloyd Wright (Frank's son; 1890-1978), whose 1926 Sowden House was a brazen, neo-Mayan concrete-block and stucco structure. Lloyd Wright's concrete-block dwelling postdated the Mayan Revival textile-block Milliard, Freeman, Storer and Ennis houses (1923-24) designed by his father in southern California; these in turn were preceded by the elder Wright's Barnsdall, or Hollyhock, House in Los Angeles (1918-21) and the Tazaemon Yamamura House in Ashiya, Japan (1918). When put together, these dwellings' blocks – with their bas-relief geometric designs – took on the aspect of an abstract frieze, visible both inside and out.

Robert B. Stacy-Judd, an architect-adventurer working in California, was much influenced by Mayan design. His largely flamboyant designs, most never realized, included a Beverly Hills home (1929) with zigzag fencing and doorway, and two humbler 1931 homes in Pismo Beach, one with a ziggurat-shaped garage, both with similarly shaped chimneys.

In Canada, the premier figure in twentieth-century Quebecois architecture was Ernest Cormier (1885-1980), whose own 1930-31 home in the Avenue des Pins, Montreal, is a fine example of an Art Deco dwelling. Although designed by a New York architect, John Walter Wood, Sherman Pratt's house (c.1931) in Niagara Island, Ontario, was a handsome mass of curves and angles, with horizontal ribbing running along its upper sections and balconies whose openwork stone edges were reminiscent of Wright's textile blocks.

A simple but elegant Art Deco residence was built in Tokyo in 1931-33 for the Crown Prince Yasuhiko Asaka, who had spent time in Paris as a student. Its outside was less high-style Gallic Art Deco than its interior spaces, but there was no mistaking its Moderne models, here transferred to a Japanese context in a beautiful garden setting.

Napier, New Zealand, a town all but destroyed by an earthquake in 1931, was the site of an ambitious new building programme resulting in domestic, civic and commercial structures in several styles, most notably Art Deco. Small-scale domestic dwellings included modest cubes with coloured mouldings, ziggurat-shaped doorways and leaded-glass windows with geometric patterns. What many consider Australia's premier Art Deco building was once a private house: Burnham Beeches, the 1933 home of Alfred Nicholas in Sherbrooke, Victoria (today a hotel). Australians refer to its design as Modern Ship Style, essentially a Streamline Moderne variant.

Apartment Houses

Multi-dwelling living units began to be built in increasing numbers, especially in the United States, in the post-Depression mid to late nineteen-thirties. Some architects responsible for Manhattan's Art Deco skyscrapers designed high-rise apartments as well, including floral, geometric and figural elements on their façades, doorways and other sections, such as lofty turrets and balconies. In other towns and cities – from Paris to Miami Beach,

An exotic female head in a Carmen Miranda-style headdress dots the lower façade of C. Christol's 1926 apartment house in 26 Avenue de Lamballe, a 16th *arrondissement* Paris street rich in Art Deco multi-dwelling residences.

San Francisco to Sydney – subtly streamlined and showy Moderne elements appeared on apartment buildings of all sizes.

Numerous nineteen-twenties apartment buildings in Paris, as well as in other French cities, were ornamented with Art Deco details, chiefly sculptures and metalwork. The 14th and 16th *arrondissements* are especially rich areas in buildings of this period. For example, the Avenue de Lamballe is dominated by multi-storey nineteen-twenties structures distinguished by their stylish decoration. Indeed, their surface motifs make up a mini-review of the Art Deco repertoire: wrought-iron doorways with roundels of bouquets; a cascading fountain on an oval stained-glass window; a floral display overflowing a giant urn in an octagonal overdoor panel; volutes and waves on a balustrade; elaborate triangular corbel pieces of dense stylized foliage and flowerheads; and exotic women's heads, clad in ornate headdresses. Dramatic Parisian housing complexes of stepped-pyramid shape were envisioned (but never built) by Henri Sauvage in the nineteen-thirties. Sauvage, whose projects defied categorization but were largely Moderne in spirit, designed an interesting artists' atelier in Auteuil (1926). Though essentially Cubist in form, its tiled façade was a play of colour, grey covering the flat areas, brown on the setback sections, polychrome on the projecting balconies.

The Amsterdam housing projects of the years immediately before and after the First World War by Piet Kramer, Michel de Klerk and others had an impact on architects worldwide, with their patterned brickwork, juxtaposition of cylindrical and cubed elements, figural sculptures, polygonal and triangular windows, prototypical streamlining and ornamental metalwork. In Dublin, for instance, architects admired the Dutch workers' housing and incorporated similar elements into their own brick structures, such as Herbert G. Simms' Sandwich Street/Hanover Street flats and his Townsend Street scheme (all 1934-36), with their setback and grooved-plaster components, arches and both rounded and pointed piers and balconies.

In England, inner-city housing was more straightforward and functionalist, although some blocks of flats were enlivened with patterned brickwork, nautically inspired balconies and Streamline Moderne entrances. Minoprion & Spenceley's 'Fairacres', Roehampton (1936), was an outstanding housing estate, a mass of curved and cylindrical elements marked by vertical fluting, and London County Council's 1928-30 Westminster Housing Scheme flats, designed by Sir Edwin Lutyens in 1936, featured unusual chequerboard façades (comprising dark brick and white plaster squares). E. Maxwell Fry's Kensal House (1937), London, planned with Elizabeth Denby as an all-encompassing 'urban village', made a strong Modernist statement, but its sweeping white curve and gridwork patterns gave it a lively emphasis not usually made by contemporary housing 'blocks'. A memorable complex of London high-rise flats was designed by Tecton's Berthold Lubetkin (1901-90): Highpoint One and Two (1933-35; 1938), in Highgate. The tall, white-washed, Cubist structures are International Style, but for the whimsical caryatids supporting the porch canopy of the later block.

The candy-coloured tones of many of Miami Beach's hotels are known to change relatively frequently, but their decorative motifs – racing stripes, stepped parapets, floral panels and porthole windows – stay the same. Among some of the resort town's jewels are four beautifully restored hotels on Ocean Drive: the Clevelander (*opposite above left*), designed by Albert Anis in 1938; the 1937 Park Central (*opposite above right*) and the 1932 Crescent (*opposite below right* and also on page 83), both by Henry Hohauser; and Roy F. France's 1936 Cavalier (*opposite below left*). Collins Avenue is the location of Henry Hohauser's vividly painted Carlton (*right below*), built in 1937, as well as the Hotel del Caribe (*right above*), which dates from 1948 but was nonetheless designed by MacKay & Gibbs in Art Deco style.

Unlike the case of Paris, where the Art Deco-decorated structures were largely *style moderne* by virtue of their ornament and not their forms (which blended in with the earlier Beaux-Arts buildings often surrounding them), in New York many apartment houses were soaring, stepped, turreted and terraced masses that stood out among their shorter neighbours. On Central Park West, massive twin-towered structures rose up in the early nineteen-thirties, two of them Art Deco masterworks from the office of Irwin Chanin: the Century Apartments (1931) and the Majestic Apartments (1930), whose upper sections were exemplary Machine Age essays with their interlocking verticals and horizontals, bands of different coloured brick and fin-like extensions. These, along with the twin-turreted Eldorado (Margon & Holder, 1931) and Emery Roth's 1931 Ardsley (which shows a Mayan influence), are arguably Manhattan's finest Art Deco apartment houses — exuberant, romantic, evocative and, seen from opposite Central Park, breathtaking.

Brightly coloured elements appeared on Manhattan high-rise apartments. At 22nd Street and Second Avenue is a 'Pueblo Deco' structure, a stepped brick mass embellished with blue and yellow terracotta. The tower of the Town House on East 38th Street (Bowden & Russell, 1930) is punctuated with polychrome terracotta, and on East 63rd Street the entrance to The Lowell (Henry S. Churchill and Herbert Lippmann, 1926) features Bertram Hartman's multi-coloured mosaic of an abstract urban landscape.

Art Deco structures were built in the Washington Heights and Inwood sections of northern Manhattan, such as H.I. Feldman's Fort Wadsworth Towers (1928) and Wadsworth Manor (1929), the latter an exuberant exercise in terracotta and brick, with distinctive triangular piers and patterned brickwork borrowed from Dutch Expressionism. Payson and Seaman Avenues contain many late nineteen-twenties and early thirties gems, their entrances decorated with Streamline Moderne, stylized floral and geometric patterns in stone and terracotta.

The other New York boroughs also reaped the benefits of the building boom; Art Deco apartments went up along Ocean Parkway, Brooklyn, and especially in the Grand Concourse-West Bronx area, where whole group-ings of Art Deco buildings appeared in the nineteen-thirties, including the sprawling 283-unit Noonan Plaza (Horace Ginsbern, 1931). Ginsbern designed over a dozen Art Deco apartment complexes in the area, with other notable structures by Israel L. Crausman, Hyman Feldman, Jacob M. Felson, H. Herbert Lilien and George W. Swiller. These stone masses were embellished with motifs drawn from the full Art Deco repertoire — Mayan, Parisian, Streamline Moderne, Machine Age, Expressionist — and at one time they made up one of the finest Art Deco neighbourhoods in the world to provide their occupants with 'the housing of the future — today'.

The most cohesive, congenial grouping of Art Deco buildings, including apartments, hotels and other structures, rose up from the nineteen-thirties onwards in Miami Beach, Florida. These were largely the work of architects Albert Anis, L. Murray Dixon, Roy F. France, Henry Hohauser and Anton

Skislewicz. Indeed, Miami Beach's well-maintained Art Deco District, which entered the American National Register of Historic Places in 1979, has become one of the prime sites to visit for enthusiasts of the style.

Most of Miami Beach's Art Deco apartment buildings sported names and were flat-roofed, straight- or curved-sided (sometimes both in one), two- or three-storey structures; many of the windows (jalousies were common) featured cantilevered sunshades. There were single buildings as well as matching pairs, either separate facing structures or connected by a centre structure at the back. The decoration on these residences was in general not as plentiful as that on the hotels, but the myriad motifs their designers employed were the same and, collectively, they comprise a rich design litany derived from numerous sources, including French, nautical, high-style New York and indigenous tropical Art Deco. Colour played an integral role, with pink, green, aqua, yellow and other shades used as highlights.

Art Deco apartment buildings appeared in other American cities, on both coasts and in the Midwest and South. In Los Angeles, Sunset Towers (Leland A. Bryant, 1929) boasted an impressive, Manhattan-style stepped silhouette awash with Art Deco motifs. In Washington, D.C., the Kennedy-Warren apartments (Joseph Younger, 1932) featured aluminium spandrels with strong Moderne motifs (somewhat at odds with griffins and other Neoclassical details on its façade). The capital's Majestic apartments (Alvin Aubinoe & Harry L. Edwards, 1937), with their ziggurat pilasters and rounded balconies, were reminiscent of many of the nineteen-thirties Art Deco residences in the Bronx (in fact, some of their standard details were mirror images of those on New York buildings).

In Napier, the rebuilt New Zealand town, low-rise residences such as the white-washed, two-storey Marine Parade Ranui Flats in the Marewa suburb, reminiscent of Miami Beach buildings, were constructed with horizontal striped highlights and decorative motifs. In Australia, the nineteen-thirties Mont St. Clair Flats, in Sydney's Darlinghurst section, comprised a sleek, seven-storey Streamline Moderne structure; except for its brick façade and height, this building, too, was akin to the sleek structures of Miami Beach Deco.

Hotels

In cities especially, the designs of hotels, apartment buildings and even skyscraper office buildings are often all but indistinguishable. In resort areas, however, hotels often take on flight-of-fancy design elements that would be anathema in other types of structures.

There were few Art Deco hotels in Paris, and those extant are fairly undistinguished, like the small, recently renovated Hôtel Parc Montsouris in the 14th *arrondissement*, its façade set with diamond-shaped panels of stylized blossoms. A gleaming Art Deco jewel on the Riviera, however, is the Martinez in Cannes. Smaller Art Deco hotels, with distinctive metalwork and sculptural elements, appeared throughout France, such as the Hôtel du Chalet in Saint-Brevin (Loire-Atlantique), the Hôtel de la Plage in Port-Mer (Ile-et-Vilaine), the Eden in Dinard and the Golf in Saint-Lunaire (Ile-et-Vilaine).

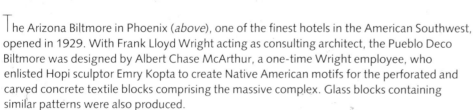

The Arizona Biltmore in Phoenix (*above*), one of the finest hotels in the American Southwest, opened in 1929. With Frank Lloyd Wright acting as consulting architect, the Pueblo Deco Biltmore was designed by Albert Chase McArthur, a one-time Wright employee, who enlisted Hopi sculptor Emry Kopta to create Native American motifs for the perforated and carved concrete textile blocks comprising the massive complex. Glass blocks containing similar patterns were also produced.

The jazzy neon signs enlivening Miami Beach's hotels at night can be as inviting and appealing as the façades seen in sun-drenched daylight. The Deco Revival palette of Henry Hohauser's 1936 Hotel Webster (*right*) is still visible in the dark, while coloured neon dramatically identifies the nocturnal Carlyle (*right above*), designed in 1941 by Kiehnel & Elliott, and Hohauser's 1932 Crescent (*opposite*).

Britain boasts several splendid Art Deco hotels. The Midland (Oliver Hill, 1932-34) in Morecambe, Lancashire, is a great white-painted-stucco-over-brick, three-storey structure whose concave-curved bulk echoes the crescent of the shore; surmounting the circular entrance tower are two massive, stylized stone sea horses by Eric Gill. Another curved structure was London's Dorchester Hotel (1930-31), to whose concrete mass (designed by Sir Owen Williams) the architect W. Curtis Green added Moderne touches, namely sculptural friezes and metalwork balconies. Geometric patterns, reminiscent of those on Amsterdam School buildings, marked the massive brick bulk of the Cumberland Hotel, London (F. J. Wills, 1933-34). Wills also designed London's Strand Palace Hotel (1929-30), whose Zigzag Moderne entrance (now removed and in the collection of the Victoria & Albert Museum) and foyer, a dazzling essay in geometry and light created by Oliver P. Bernard, was one of the finest examples of high-style Art Deco in Britain. On the southern coast, in Bigbury-on-Sea, South Devon, the Burgh Island Hotel (Matthew Dawson, 1929) is a 'white palace' inside and out, with prow-like jutting balconies, stained-glass Peacock Dome and a pleasing combination of curves and straight lines. A colourful exuberance marked Glasgow's superb Beresford Hotel (James W. Weddell, 1938). The Streamline Moderne façade of the massive block, called 'Glasgow's first skyscraper hotel' at the time of its opening, was sheathed with red, black and mustard-gold faience.

American Art Deco hotels were found in both urban and resort areas. The golden-brick Panhellenic Hotel (John Mead Howells, 1929-30) was Manhattan's first skyscraper hotel, but the most glittering was the Waldorf-Astoria (Schultze & Weaver, 1931), a twin-towered, multi-setback limestone structure.

Most of the characteristics of Miami Beach's apartment buildings applied to the resort city's hotels. The ornamental motifs were much the same, the colour highlights as bold, but there were considerably more elements: more storeys, more elaborate signage and more neon. Some, like the Ritz Plaza, Delano, St Moritz and Shelborne, were over ten storeys high, and many shorter structures featured smart vertical beacons crowning their tops or clinging to their fronts. Curving around 9th Street at Ocean Drive was the Waldorf Towers (Albert Anis, 1937), punctuated on the corner by a cylindrical lookout tower, and two blocks south were three contiguous gems: the Majestic (Albert Anis, 1940), Imperial (L. Murray Dixon, 1939) and Park Central (Henry Hohauser, 1937) hotels, whose façades present a harmonious blend of shapes and motifs: circular, foliate, octagonal, chevron, and horizontal and vertical, with ubiquitous eyebrows over the windows. Dozens more Art Deco hotels occupied Ocean Drive and Collins Avenue, their rectilinear, streamlined façades marked by similar standard motifs, as well as the occasional unique one, such as the Marlin (L. Murray Dixon, 1939), set with marine bas-reliefs.

Many other American towns boasted one or more Art Deco hotels. In Atlantic City, for example, there was the four-storey Hotel Apollo of 1926,

The most glittering Art Deco hotel in Manhattan was the Waldorf-Astoria, designed by Schultze & Weaver in 1931. The Park Avenue and 49th Street structure easily rivalled nearby 'cathedrals of commerce', as well as hotels all over the globe; indeed, at the time it was built the 47-storey Waldorf was the world's largest hotel. Especially noteworthy were the zigzag lines highlighting the domes of the twin turrets and the wealth of ornamental metalwork in the Moderne vein.

One of the most flamboyant designs of the British-born adventurer-architect, Robert B. Stacy-Judd, was the 1925 Aztec Hotel in Monrovia, California, parts of whose façade were densely decorated with abstract Mayan symbols and geometric motifs.

its façade a lively geometric essay on the arc and semicircle, as well as the coloured stucco-sheathed Atlantic Beach Club (Joseph Urban), a rectangular mass enhanced by white, gold and rose facing. In Liberal, Kansas, the Hotel Warren was literally covered with Deco motifs, and in Fort Worth, the Blackstone Hotel (Mauran, Russell & Crowell, with Elmer G. Withers, 1929) was a stepped-back, reinforced-concrete, stone and brick mass that qualified as the Texas city's first Art Deco skyscraper.

The parapet of the Clovis Hotel in Clovis, New Mexico (Robert Merrell, 1931), was decorated with the busts of fourteen noble Plains Indians in full war-bonnet regalia, each capping a stepped concrete pier embellished with incised geometric and stylized-floral motifs. The eleven-storey, buff-brick building was for a time the state's tallest. In Phoenix, the Arizona Biltmore (1929), often attributed to Frank Lloyd Wright, was in fact designed by Albert Chase McArthur (Wright was a consultant on the project). McArthur hired a Hopi sculptor, Emry Kopta, to design the Biltmore's distinctive concrete textile blocks, whose rectangular forms, with carved and perforated decoration, were also made in moulded glass. Not only is the unevenly massed building itself a triumph of Pueblo Deco, but so are ancillary areas, such as the swimming pool and patio. In California, the exterior of Robert B. Stacy-Judd's Aztec Hotel in Monrovia (1925) was a dense carpet of abstract Mayan symbols and geometric motifs, while the Lafayette Hotel in Long Beach (Schilling & Schilling c.1930-31) was a handsome Moderne slab of concrete and terracotta, its leitmotif the zigzag.

Several notable Art Deco hotels were built in the Pacific. An Australian chip-off-the-Miami-block, with a nod to English Odeons, was built in Clifton Hill, Victoria, in the nineteen-thirties: the two-storey, flat-roofed United Kingdom Hotel featured streamlined corners, stripes of varicoloured bricks, nautical railings along the wraparound balcony and a monolithic stepped pilaster rising over the doorway. In Napier, New Zealand, the Masonic Hotel (W.J. Prouse, 1932) was a broad, two-storey, white-washed hotel with a distinctive doorway, and the Hotel Central (E.A. Williams, 1931) featured sunburst transoms and zigzag motifs.

Even as far afield as Bandung, West Java, there were the stepped Moderne Isola – a private villa turned deluxe hotel – and the Savoy Homann Hotel (1938), a long, low structure with streamlined corners, a sleek, squared-off tower and a distinct Dutch Expressionist influence.

Several Art Deco hotels were built in Shanghai, a popular stop on the itinerary of sophisticated Western travellers. The Jingjiang (1931) was once a private hotel for French residents, and the Peace Hotel, built by Sir Victor Sassoon in the late nineteen-twenties as the Cathay (Noel Coward wrote *Private Lives* there in 1929), was the city's most splendid pre-Revolution hotel. The Shanghai Mansions, a residential hotel built in 1934 as the Broadway Mansions, was a 22-storey, red-brick structure in the stepped skyscraper mode.

Chapter 5

Public Buildings

In the nineteen-twenties and thirties, especially in the United States, the number of civic, commercial, ecclesiastical and other public structures built in various Art Deco styles – from Mayan Revival to Streamline Moderne, low-rise industrial-design to high-style Parisian – was considerable. In small towns and large cities alike, Art Deco structures rose as offices, factories and restaurants. Many such buildings were built under public agency schemes, such as the Works Progress Administration, started in 1935.

Office Buildings:
from Low-rise Masses to Skyscrapers

For many, the quintessential Art Deco building is the soaring New York skyscraper. The appeal of these symbols of a new age and optimism is undeniable, as is their premier place on the roster of Art Deco architecture. The skyscraper as such, however, was not born in twenties Manhattan, but in the Chicago of the eighteen-nineties; nor did it thrive only in the United States. Skyscrapers could be hotels, apartments and department stores, although their most prominent role was as nine-to-five 'cathedrals of commerce'. Vertical masses were not the only kind of large commercial or business structure either: offices could also be housed in low-rise edifices, as they most often were in smaller cities and medium-sized towns throughout Europe, North America, Australia and elsewhere.

Art Deco office buildings were not as commonplace in Europe as in North America, and there were no examples of skyscrapers. In the Hague, J.J.P. Oud's massive Shell Building (1938-42), though verging on functionalism and far from the architect's De Stijl-influenced projects, was marked by Streamline Moderne and decorative elements, notably in the scallop shells amid a sea of geometric motifs above the entrance. The Shell Building (L. Bechmann & Chatenay, 1932) in Paris was significant, too, because its crisp, rectilinear corner design was informed by the style of New York office buildings. The 1933 edifice by Raymond Février in the Rue de Châteaudun showed its New York roots in stepped segments and spandrels. On a seven-storey office building (Alex and Pierre Fournier, 1929) in the Rue Pasquier, once home of the Société Financière Française et Coloniale and now the Bayerische Vereinsbank S.A., the façade was brightened by G. Saupique's stylized animals in coloured marble, enamel and mosaic. In the Rue La Fayette, a fabled phoenix, stylized sunrays and Moderne lettering were incised in amber-hued stone over the entry of the Phénix insurance building (F. Balleyguier, 1932).

Opposite

The sparkling spire of New York's Chrysler Building (William Van Alen, 1928-31), with the 59th-floor chromium nickel-steel eagle gargoyles visible at its foot.

Although none qualified as a skyscraper, several notable office and commercial structures were built in London. Ideal House of 1928 in Argyll Street was an Anglo-American project by Raymond Hood and Gordon Jeeves; its exotic polychrome elements on a black ground made the building a splendid jewel in its largely neo-Tudor/Neoclassical surroundings. Another black-sheathed structure struck a different note: the subtly stepped Daily Express Building (Sir E. Owen Williams, with Ellis & Clarke, 1930-32) in Fleet Street. The sleek façade of this curved corner edifice, which originally housed offices as well as printing plant, was made up of black Vitrolite and glass. Four massive stone piles enlivened with Moderne elements, mostly sculptural, were the London Passenger Transport Board (Adams, Holden & Pearson, 1926-29), Broadcasting House (Val Myer, 1930-32), Unilever House (J. Lomax Simpson with Sir John Burnet, 1930-32) and the massive stepped Shell Mex House (Messrs Joseph, 1931-32). H.S. Goodhart-Rendel's head office for the Hay's Wharf Company (1928-32) was a glittering box on steel *pilotis*, its Thameside façade adorned with handsome lettering and gilded ceramic figural reliefs by Frank Dobson. Possibly the last gasp of the Moderne in Britain was Albert Lakeman's 1937-39 Imperial Airways Building (later B.O.A.C. and British Airways headquarters), a huge stone structure with a concave-curved front, stepped clock tower and, over the entry, a pair of stylized-winged figures.

The skyscraper was *the* definitive Art Deco office building in Manhattan. In Lower Manhattan, the Barclay-Vesey Building (Ralph T. Walker, 1889-1973, for McKenzie, Voorhees & Gmelin, 1923-26) was the first important Art Deco office building. Although much of its bas-relief ornament – vines, grapes and flowers around the phone company's bell over the main entrance, for instance – is curvilinear, naturalistic and more akin to Art Nouveau, the stepped mass of the structure is boldly modern. A cousin of the Barclay-Vesey is Walker's 1928 Chesapeake and Potomac Telephone Company in Washington, its bas-reliefs still a sea of interlacing tendrils, but now with Moderne stepped and fluted pilasters.

The American Radiator Building (Raymond M. Hood, 1881-1934, for Hood, Godley & Fouilhoux, 1924) does not feature Moderne decoration, but the skyscraper's black-brick skin is bejewelled with gold neo-Gothic trimmings and presages Hood's later polychrome Art Deco towers. Hood's two other major New York projects were the News Building (Howells & Hood, 1929-30) and the McGraw-Hill Building (Hood, Godley & Fouilhoux, 1930-31).

Hood was also the guiding spirit behind the Associated Architects consortium responsible for Rockefeller Center, the massive, multi-faceted complex that rose up between Fifth and Sixth Avenues and West 48th and 51st Streets from 1931 to 1940. Comprising the RCA and other high- and low-rise offices, Radio City Music Hall, shops, restaurants, a sunken plaza and sculpture gardens, Rockefeller Center is a glittering urban showpiece. Its fourteen original limestone piles are set with metal spandrels and highlighted with gilded and polychrome sculpture. These decorative

The subtly stepped, streamlined form of the Daily Express Building (Sir Owen Williams, with Ellis & Clarke, 1930-32), in London's Fleet Street, was clad in shiny black Vitrolite and glass.

elements, which serve to both embellish and unify the buildings, are largely majestic Art Deco images allegorical in nature, and they were created by leading sculptors, including René Paul Chambellan, Leo Friedlander, Alfred-Auguste Janniot, Carl Paul Jennewein, Lee Lawrie, Paul Manship, Hildreth Meiere and Carl Milles.

The New York firm of Ralph T. Walker (Voorhees, Gmelin & Walker, formerly McKenzie, Voorhees & Gmelin) created some of New York's most exuberant Art Deco structures, many with zigzag decoration. The Amsterdam School-inspired Western Union Building (1928-30), in Hudson Street, was clad in bricks that shaded through twenty-one colour variations, and over its three dramatic proscenium-like entryways were brick and bronze arches of concertina form. The firm designed several New York Telephone Company buildings, including three in Manhattan (1929-30) and the Long Island Area Headquarters in Brooklyn (1931); their decoration was mostly geometric in nature, but the West 50th Street building also included stylized-willow bas-reliefs. The irregular mass of Salvation Army Buildings (1929-30) in West 14th Street featured a soaring entryway, with stepped segments and ornamental metalwork. Two of the firm's projects in upstate New York were the Genesee Valley Trust Building (c.1929) in Rochester (now the Times Square Building), with its wing-capped spire, and New York Telephone in Syracuse (c.1929), its bas-reliefs reminiscent of those on the Barclay-Vesey Building.

Ely Jacques Kahn (1884-1972) was responsible for over three dozen commercial structures in New York, nearly all of them marked, inside and out, by a distinctive geometric vocabulary – jazzy, dynamic patterns rendered in bronze, brick and terracotta, the latter often in vivid colours. Indeed, Kahn's projects are renowned for their detailed, decorative parts, rather than the sum of their form and ornament. Among his significant creations were 2 Park Avenue (1927), a brick box with Mayan-type motifs; the Film Center (1928-29); the Squibb Building (1929-30); the Holland Plaza Building (1930); and 120 Wall Street (1930).

The firm of A. Stewart Walker and Leon Gillette produced several distinctive Art Deco structures. The Fuller Building (1928-29), in East 57th Street, was a white-brick, setback tower with black details, its top embellished with zigzag and sun-like patterns of vaguely Aztec origin, its entryway dominated by an octagonal clock and figures by Elie Nadelman. Monumental sculptures marked Joseph Urban's Hearst Magazine Building (1927-28), which was inspired by classical sources, filtered through Vienna Secession rather than high-style Paris. Six columns extend above the six-storey mass; atop them are zigzag-decorated urns, while below them are positioned two figures.

The neo-Gothic top of Cross & Cross's RCA Victor Building (1930-31) is the only retrospective element of this office tower. The structure's dizzying façade is set with zigzag thunderbolts, scrolls, upwards-pointing hands and, way above the fifty-one storeys, a lacy stone setting for dramatic masks wearing elaborate Mayan-like headdresses.

Near Grand Central Station, Sloan & Robertson's 1926-27 Graybar Building (*left above* and *below*) features dramatic bas-reliefs of classical gods on its Lexington Avenue façade, and the old Oakland Floral Depot (*above*), designed by Albert Evers in 1931, sparkles in a coat of silver and blue terracotta.

Shades of blue also dominate the two structures (*opposite*): Harry Sternfeld and Gabriel Roth's 1928 WCAU Building in Philadelphia (*below*), which is studded with electric-volt-like metal bands on its cladding of blue-glass chips set in plastic, and Claude Beelman's International Center in downtown Los Angeles (*above*), opened in 1930 as the Bankers Building.

The skyscrapers that best exemplify Art Deco New York are the Chanin, Chrysler and Empire State buildings. The Chanin, at 122 East 42nd Street, dates from 1928-29 and was designed by Sloan & Robertson, with input from owner Irwin S. Chanin. It is a stepped fifty-six storey structure whose lower sections are alive with bronze patterned spandrels, other metal segments and terracotta bas-reliefs. Three storeys above ground level is a rich ten-foot-high band of floral and foliate bas-reliefs, below which are sculpted spandrels, pier caps and more bands whose subjects, including fans, dragons, masks, zigzags and waterfowl, make a heady hotchpotch. The exterior and interior ornament was designed by Jacques L. Delamarre, in collaboration with René Paul Chambellan.

The stainless steel-arched, triangular-windowed spire of the Chrysler Building (William Van Alen, 1928-31) is a Manhattan landmark. Although the seventy-seven storey building's height has long been surpassed, its sparkling beauty – part folly and fantasy, part advertising motif, but part functional office tower as well – has yet to be. The Chrysler's façade, which is basically white brick with grey trim, is punctuated with bold, jazzy ornament: chromium nickel-steel Moderne eagle gargoyles on the 59th floor; metal hubcaps in the centre of car-wheel designs in coloured brick on the 31st floor, leading to dual-winged forms, like hood ornaments, at the corners; and similar aluminium flagpole sockets with winged-head forms.

The Chrysler's claim to being the world's tallest building was outstripped in barely a year by the mammoth limestone, granite, aluminium and nickel structure piercing the horizon eight blocks south, the Empire State Building (Shreve, Lamb & Harmon, 1930-31). Notwithstanding its long-unrivalled height of 102 stories, the Empire State is more than just a symbol of New York: it is an elegant stepped structure of subtle but strong ornamentation: Moderne eagles over the entrance, cast-metal spandrels, four wing-like extensions clinging to the aluminium mast at its peak and pinnate 'capitals' atop lower-level pilasters. Another Shreve, Lamb & Harmon project was the building at 500 Fifth Avenue (1930-31), with smoky-black terracotta spandrels defining the vertical mid-section of its buff terracotta face and an entryway sparkling with gilded bas-reliefs. The firm also designed the Reynolds Tobacco Company headquarters in Winston-Salem, North Carolina, a twenty-plus-storey building of stepped section and ornament.

Multi-storey and low-rise office buildings sprouted up throughout the United States from the late nineteen-twenties. None was as dramatic as the Chrysler nor as tall as the Empire State, but many became well-known and much-loved landmarks.

In Syracuse, New York, the Niagara Mohawk Power Corporation Building (Melvin L. King, with Bley & Lyman, 1930-32) rivalled the Chrysler in terms of the shiny metal on its limestone façade. Dominating the uppermost cresting was 'The Spirit of Light', Clayton Frye's stainless steel figure, a powerful machine-aesthetic rendering of the human form.

In Connecticut, the Southern New England Telephone Company buildings in Hartford (R. W. Foote, 1930) and New Haven (R. W. Foote &

The ornate entrance to Rubush & Hunter's Circle Tower Building in Indianapolis (1929-30) includes a carved limestone arch and bronze grille. The dominant theme is Egyptian, with motifs such as papyrus and lotus blossoms, scarab beetles and assorted Pharaonic figures.

Douglas Orr, 1937) featured smart Moderne elements. A zigzag leitmotif occurred on bands of both the metal grillework and stone sculpture of the Hartford building, as well as plentiful scrolls, chevrons and stylized flowers. In New Haven the prominent bas-relief ornament over the entrance was allegorical and classical. Elsewhere in the country, many telephone company structures sported Art Deco motifs.

Of the office buildings constructed in the Washington area in the nineteen-thirties, most (such as the Heurich Building on K Street, N.W.) were of a rather sober, classical mien as indeed were many structures in the capital, notably civic ones. Lively exceptions were two complementary buildings commissioned by the Brownley's confection company and built by Porter & Lockie in F Street, N.W., in 1932. The façade of the latter building, which featured a Brownley's store at street level, was covered with typical Deco motifs: zigzags, sunbursts and stylized flowers and scrolls.

Several prominent Art Deco office buildings helped define the growing skyline of Philadelphia (though, in accordance with a gentlemen's agreement, none rose higher than the cast-iron statue of William Penn crowning the Beaux-Arts City Hall). Ralph B. Bencker designed the thirteen-storey buff and limestone headquarters of N.W. Ayer & Son, the advertising firm (1927-29), whose façade was rich in symbolic sculpture. Along the upper three floors were figural pylons representing Truth, each holding an open book, and the spandrels below the topmost windows comprised groups relating to the advertising business. The form and decoration of the WCAU Building (Harry Sternfeld & Gabriel Roth, 1928) could be likened to a huge expressive radio wave: at the top was a bold glass tower, which glowed blue at night when the radio station was on the air. The lower-level and upper ziggurat of the Market Street National Bank (Ritter & Shay, 1930), now One East Penn Square, was awash with Mayan Revival motifs, including necklace-like swags of turquoise, orange and white terracotta. Paul Philippe Cret's Integrity Trust Company (c.1931) had a handsome black granite entrance with a scalloped design at the top; the same motif was echoed on the metal lamps attached to the building along street level. The Philadelphia Savings Fund Society (Howe & Lescaze, 1930-32) was a sign of things to come: the PSFS tower is deemed by many the first American International Style skyscraper, although the highly polished grey-granite base, its corners curved, can legitimately be considered vestigial Streamline Moderne.

The ornamented skyscraper first saw the light of day in eighteen-nineties Chicago, where several Art Deco buildings were later constructed. The Merchandise Mart (Graham, Anderson, Probst & White, 1929-30) was acclaimed for its limestone mass rather than height; until the Pentagon was built, it was the world's largest structure. Its style was quietly modern, its stepped volume the most salient feature. On the other hand, the Palmolive Building (Holabird & Root, 1929-30) was a soaring structure of six setback sections; its decoration was simplified and unshowy, largely in the guise of vertical grooves cutting their way down the sides of this mass of masonry.

Manhattan's Rockefeller Center (1931-40) is a huge commercial precinct whose somewhat daunting masses of stone are, at their lower levels, enhanced by a variety of allegorical sculptures – from polychrome bas-reliefs to huge gilded figures. Prominent sculptors from several countries were engaged to create these works of art, which included Hildreth Meiere's roundels of Drama, Dance and Song (*left top to bottom*) on the facade of Radio City Music Hall and, on the International Building, a group of fifteen limestone bas-relief 'hieroglyphs' representing the four races of Man, as well as aspects of Art, Science, Trade and Industry, all by Lee Lawrie (*above*). Paul Manship's massive gilt-bronze *Prometheus* dominates the sunken plaza in front of the high-rise RCA Building (*opposite*).

Nearly the same can be said of Holabird & Root's Riverside Plaza (1929), the old Chicago Daily News Building, which had been erected 'as a symbol of the triumph of modern journalism'. A virtually undecorated, symmetrical slab form, with vault-like side entrances, the wide mass is set off by stepped sections at the top and ubiquitous vertical bands serving as *faux*-pilasters. The topmost feature of Holabird & Root's Chicago Board of Trade (1930) was the sleek tower's most Moderne component: John Storrs' cast-chromium-plated steel sculpture of a faceless Ceres, a sack of money in her right hand, a sheaf of wheat in her left. Chicago's finest Art Deco skyscraper in terms of decoration was the Carbide and Carbon Building (D.H. Burnham & Co., *c.*1929), called 'the first all-terracotta skyscraper in color' in a Northwestern Terra Cotta Company advertisement.

In Detroit, two densely ornamented structures, the Fisher Building (Albert Kahn, 1928) and the Union Trust Company Building (Wirt Rowland, with Smith, Hinchman & Grylls, 1929), featured ambitious arrays of sculptural and other motifs, inside and out. Skilled craftsmen were engaged to decorate the Fisher Building (commissioned by the Fisher brothers of the Fisher Body Company), a massive complex that included a thirty-six-storey central office tower, shops, a Mayan Revival cinema and two eleven-storey wings and a parking garage that could hold 1,100 cars.

A building boom in Kansas City during the nineteen-twenties and thirties resulted in a sudden spate of commercial buildings in the Art Deco style or embellished with Moderne elements. The Kansas City Power and Light Company Building (Hoit, Price & Barnes, 1932) was a gleaming gem, whose sunburst and scrolled tower was topped by a glazed pyramid that glowed orange. The oil-rich city of Tulsa also boasted many Art Deco structures, including the First National Bank (Weary & Allford, 1932), with a florid, Parisian-influence aluminium entrance, George Winkler's Public Service Company Office and the Medical Arts Building (1928). Although built in 1956, the Price Tower, Frank Lloyd Wright's copper, glass, concrete and steel skyscraper in Bartlesville, Oklahoma, was the much-modified actualization of a 1929 concept. Its profuse use of glass puts it firmly in the nineteen-fifties, but its decoration and silhouette relate it to earlier skyscrapers.

Commercial Art Deco structures were built throughout the South, Southwest and West, from the sixteen-storey Medical Arts Building (1929) in Hot Springs, Arkansas, to the Threefoot Building in Meridian, Mississippi (C.H. Lindsley, *c.*1930), its entrance awash with terracotta scrolls, sunbursts and zigzags in seven colours. In Phoenix, there were two notable Art Deco structures. The twelve-storey, stucco-clad Luhrs Tower (Trost & Trost, 1930), considered the only Pueblo Deco skyscraper, was embellished at its top with green terracotta ornament in the form of stylized plants and the busts of Spanish conquistadors. The Valley Bank and Trust Company (Morgan, Walls & Clements with H.H. Green, 1932) was a sober limestone and concrete mass, its decoration comprising two Moderne eagles over the door and a mélange of classic-Deco motifs – scrolls, foliage, zigzags and stepped, fluted sections – on the roof, spandrels and pilasters.

California, notably Los Angeles, followed New York in terms of the quantity of Art Deco office buildings, although none approached Manhattan's skyscrapers in size. In San Francisco, the Medical and Dental Building (Miller & Pflueger, 1930) in Sutter Street was a gem of Mayan Revival architecture, its entrance a dense mosaic of Meso-American-derived figures and symbols. Two of Los Angeles' finest treasures were the Richfield Oil (later Atlantic Richfield, or ARCO) and Eastern Columbia buildings. The former (Morgan, Walls & Clements, 1928-29) was covered in glazed black and gold terracotta and surmounted by a tower of lacy metalwork. Along the parapet and over the doorway were gilded-terracotta figures by Haig Patigian representing motive power. The Eastern Columbia Building (Claude Beelman, 1930) originally housed four floors of selling space as well as offices, auditorium, lunch room and other staff areas. A clock tower made up the uppermost section of the building, which was sheathed in blue-green terracotta punctuated with gilding.

In other North and South American countries, architects created Art Deco buildings inspired by American as well as European designs, but often incorporating native motifs. In post-revolutionary Mexico, Modernism generally held sway over Art Deco, but some stepped office towers, by architects such as Juan O'Gorman (1905-82), were built, their designs representing a midpoint between the dying Beaux-Arts tradition and nascent Modernism. Two stepped office towers were built in Buenos Aires, the Edificio Kavanagh (Sánchez, Lagos y de la Torre, 1934) and the Edificio Safico (1932), built under the direction of the civil engineer Walter Möll. The latter was topped with a ziggurat form as close to its Mayan source as possible, in that the top six floors were separately stepped.

In Canada Ernest I. Barott and Ernest Cormier were two prominent architects, some of whose designs incorporated Art Deco motifs. The former's firm, Barott & Blackader, was responsible for the Bank of Montreal in Ottawa (1930-34), a classical pile whose ambitious Moderne sculpture programme by Emil Siebern included allegorical figures of Prosperity, Thrift, Industry and Forests. The Calgary and Halifax branches of the Bank of Nova Scotia featured a wealth of bas-reliefs of stylized Canadian flora, fauna and marine life.

The old state Maritime Services Board in Sydney, Australia, designed by William Withers in the thirties (but not built until 1952), was an H-shaped stone pile with a stepped tower in the middle. This ersatz office building is now the Museum of Contemporary Art.

Napier, New Zealand, is not without some notable office and related commercial buildings. The white-faced Daily Telegraph Building (E.A. Williams, 1932) is an elegant, symmetrical structure, and the retail-cum-office Smith and Chambers Building (H. Alfred Hill, 1932), today the Kidsons Building, features prominent bands of zigzags on its façade. The Bank of New Zealand Building (Crichton, McKay & Haughton, 1932) contains both Moderne zigzag decoration and a similar stylized Maori pattern (called 'kowhaiwhai').

Frank Lloyd Wright's 1929 drawing for the St Mark's Tower project in New York was the basis of the 1953-56 H. C. Price Company office-apartment building in Bartlesville, Oklahoma. The master himself wrote of the 19-storey copper, glass, concrete and steel building, 'Now the skyscraper comes into its own in the rolling plains of Oklahoma'.

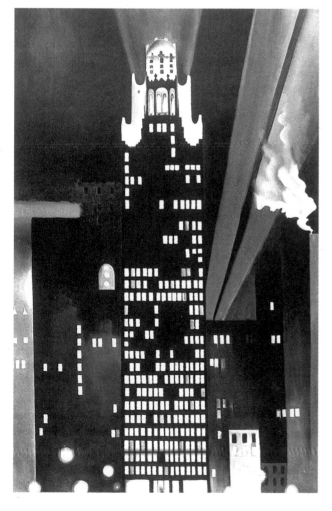

The blue-green terracotta-clad Eastern Columbia Building in Los Angeles (*opposite*), designed by Claude Beelman and dating from 1930, was an unlikely – yet somehow apposite – setting for the 1991 film *Predator 2* (*above left*). At the other end of the aesthetic spectrum, painter Georgia O'Keeffe was taken enough by the sheer beauty of the 1924 American Radiator (now American-Standard) Building in Manhattan (*above*) – shown here in a painting by Birch Burdette Long – to execute it in oil in 1927 (*left*). The crown of the black-brick 40 West 40th Street building, which was Raymond M. Hood's first major New York project, was capped with gold terracotta.

American workplaces of the nineteen-twenties and
thirties were not all in the vertical skyscraper mode, as the
two low structures (*opposite*) illustrate. Frank Lloyd
Wright's S.C. Johnson and Son administration offices in
Racine, Wisconsin (*above*), dated from 1936-39 (the tower
is from 1947-50) and comprised a sprawl of artfully linked
buildings made of brick, glass and translucent plastic tubing.
The John C. Austin Co. was responsible for the now
demolished Radio City (*below*), NBC's 1938-39
broadcasting headquarters in Hollywood.

One of the few all-colour Manhattan skyscrapers was the
1930-31 McGraw-Hill Building in East 42nd Street (*right*),
designed by Raymond M. Hood. The bulk of the 35-storey
office tower was sheathed with greenish-blue terracotta
that shaded to blue at the top, and the entrance was made
up of horizontal bands in white, green and blue with
vermilion highlights.

Sloan & Robertson's 1928-29 Chanin Building (*below*) featured an ambitious decorative programme (by Jacques Delamarre and René Paul Chambellan) both inside and out; this purported to tell the tale of the 'City of Opportunity', but the floral, geometric, avian and other subjects seen on the structure's East 42nd Street façade are rather confusing, although handsomely executed. More coherent, apposite – and optimistic – are the decorative terracotta panels adorning the façade of the Depression-era Laramie State Bank in Chicago (*above*), showing the public reaping the benefits of their hard work.

But for the wing-like extensions clinging to its aluminium mast and a pair of Moderne eagles guarding its entrance, the subtly stepped Empire State Building (*opposite*) is surprisingly bereft of external ornament.

Stepped masses of brick and stone, with a variety of decorative touches, comprised the bulk of commercial buildings in the Art Deco style. One of the finest was the Niagara Hudson Power Company (*above*) in upstate Syracuse, New York, notable for the gleaming metal on its limestone façade; a prominent feature was Clayton Frye's stainless steel sculpture, the winged 'Spirit of Light', which stood guard high over the entrance. A significant metal component, a tower of lacy metalwork, likewise crowned the 1928-29 Atlantic Richfield Building in Los Angeles (*right*), designed by Morgan, Walls & Clements. The building also featured Haig Patigian's winged figures, symbolic of motive power. The decoration on Ralph T. Walker's 1923-26 New York Telephone (or Barclay-Vesey) Building in Lower Manhattan (*opposite*) – the city's first significant Art Deco office tower – is less striking from a distance; it largely consists of blossoms, vines and figures more akin to Art Nouveau and Arts and Crafts designs rather than Moderne motifs.

104

Handsome or ingenious decorative details on Art Deco high-rises often go unappreciated, because they can only be best seen in an aerial view or from an upper floor of a nearby building. The Mayan-derived swags bedecking the façade of Ritter & Shay's Market Street National Bank Building (now One East Penn Square) in Philadelphia (*left*) are executed in brightly hued terracotta, and a medieval castle-like array of stepped archways and piers set the stage for the observation deck of New York's 1928-29 Chanin Building (*left below*), by Sloan & Robertson.

Although at first glance the tower of Cross & Cross's 1931 RCA Building (*opposite*) may appear largely neo-Gothic, a closer look reveals a plethora of Art Deco details, from allegorical and stylized figures to thunderbolts and zigzags. In fact, the motifs were meant to represent radio waves — symbols that are not inappropriate for the structure's present incarnation as the General Electric Building.

The chiaroscuro works of New York architectural artist Hugh Ferriss (1889-1962) presented portraits of buildings intended, realized and imagined. His *oeuvre* not only indicated a talented artist with a unique style and vision, but also helped define a certain heady period in urban America. Ferriss's (*left*) 1930 perspective in charcoal on board of the proposed Majestic Hotel on New York's Upper West Side was done for the Chanin Architectural Office.

Hugh Ferriss's collection of drawings, gathered together and published in 1929 as *The Metropolis of Tomorrow*, included examples of actual, visionary and 'deconstructed' (that is, shown in initial planning and building stages) architecture. 'Overhead Traffic-Ways' wherein 'all "setbacks" of buildings have been aligned and made into automobile highways' are shown in the drawing (*above*). The 'Fourth Stage' in the 'Evolution of the Set-Back Building' (*opposite*) presents a pure shape devoid of decoration but, in the artist's words, a 'practical, basic form for large buildings'.

Though it was designed by William Henry Withers in the late thirties, the old state Maritime Services Board Building in Sydney (*left*) was not constructed until 1952; nonetheless, it still qualifies as one of the country's finest Moderne structures. Today, this H-shaped golden-brick pile is the Museum of Contemporary Art. To the right of the museum is the great architectural-engineering feat, the Sydney Harbour Bridge, whose stepped pylons are in the Moderne vein. Dating from 1923-32, the span was designed by Dorman Long & Co. Ltd. of Middlesbrough, England.

This 1929 Paris building (*above*) was originally the home of the Société Financière Française et Coloniale, and its façade was embellished with Georges Saupique's elegantly stylized coloured enamel, marble and mosaic animals (the beasts were indigenous to various French colonies). Designed by Alex and Pierre Fournier and located in the Rue Pasquier in the 9th *arrondissement*, the building today houses the Bayerische Vereinsbank.

The Daily Telegraph Building in Napier, New Zealand (*below*), presents a crisp, white-washed Neoclassical-Moderne face. It was designed by E.A. Williams in 1932 and is one of the finest Art Deco structures of the town.

Multi-stepped high-rise masses were built in several countries in the thirties. Sometimes they were liberally embellished with sculptural decoration, as on Gordon B. Kaufmann's 1931-35 Los Angeles Times Building (*opposite*), whereas other structures, like Adams, Holden & Pearson's 1926-29 London Passenger Transport Board (*left*), were only lightly sprinkled with ornament (in this case sculptures by Jacob Epstein, Eric Gill and the young Henry Moore). The rectilinear forms of two Mexico City skyscrapers (*above*), the Goodrich Tyre and National Lottery buildings at the intersection of the Avenida Juarez and Paseo de la Reforma, signal the movement towards the International Style.

Ralph T. Walker of the New York architectural firm of Voorhees, Gmelin & Walker created the 1930 Genesee Valley Trust Company (now Times Square) Building in Rochester, New York (*left*). Above the first-floor façade windows are carved stone panels by Leo Friedlander, and a stylized floral leitmotif occurs both inside and out. The building's crowning glory is its massive signal tower, topped by four huge aluminium wings. Known locally as 'the wings of progress', these alate forms make a bold aerodynamic and Streamline Moderne statement.

The curved mass of BBC's Broadcasting House (*opposite*), dating from 1930-32 and designed by G. Val Myer, was studded with sculptural elements by Eric Gill and Vernon Hill. A contemporary reviewer said it divided the roadway 'like a battleship floating towards the observer', and in the main its Moderne aspects were thought excessive by contemporary critics.

Factories, warehouses, power stations, printing plants and other edifices whose inner function was all-important had outer forms designed in the Art Deco style during the twenties and thirties. Whether white-washed masses with polychrome-terracotta touches or sleek stone and glass blocks with streamlined corners, these structures provided a pleasing image for clients, passers-by and even workers. They also helped to humanize the all-too-often harsh, brutal picture of industry, and alter the commonly held image of bleak, grimy Victorian-era factories.

Beginning with Peter Behrens' A.E.G. turbine factory in west Berlin (1908-09), and Walter Gropius' and Adolf Meyer's Fagus Factory near Hildesheim (1911), industrial structures became more than faceless masses of brick, metal and glass; indeed, they metamorphosed into modern temples of production that were worthy of architectural greatness as commercial structures.

The United Kingdom was especially rich in Moderne industrial buildings. Of major importance was the London Power Company's Battersea Power Station (S.L. Pearce, engineer; Halliday & Agate, with Sir Giles Gilbert Scott, 1930-34), with its extraordinary silhouette of fluted chimneys on stepped bases of vertically textured brick. Called a 'futurist icon' and 'new cathedral', the electricity-generating station was once Britain's prime symbol of modernity and progress, admired by many as the foremost example of 'modern architecture for modern industry' and as a 'successful architectural solution of what is primarily an engineering problem'. Other such impressive engineering-architectural efforts included the Derby Power Station (Arthur Easton & Son), the filtration plant of the Metropolitan Water Board in Kempton (H.E. Stilgoe, chief engineer) and Herbert J. Rowse's six brick ventilation stations for the 1934 Mersey Tunnel in Liverpool, with their Moderne sculptural decoration.

Without doubt, the finest group of Art Deco factories was designed by Wallis, Gilbert & Partners, London. The Hoover Factory (1932) in Perivale, Middlesex, was the most distinguished of these, but the Firestone (1929) and Pyrene (1930) buildings in Brentford were handsome as well. Before this London trio, however, there was the Wrigley's factory in North Wembley (*c.*1926-27), a long white structure whose stepped sides, with fluted cornices, looked forward to the other factories, distinguished by their polychrome faience tiles against white-washed backgrounds. The Firestone Tyre Factory, a steel-framed structure of reinforced concrete, had the basic form of a classical temple, with a long stepped causeway at the front that led to the main entrance. Its façade decoration surrounded the front door and capped the capitals and bases of the fluted pilasters making up the colonnade. Sources for its decoration were various, including Egyptian, Greek, Moorish and even Native American. The Pyrene Building was less classical and more zigzag Moderne, its jazzy angular metalwork especially notable. The firm's 1932 brick and concrete design for London's Hall & Co. also contained ornate Moderne metalwork, and its door frames were shaped like Egyptian pylons. The Hoover Factory was Wallis, Gilbert's *tour*

A smart, angular clock tower embellished the centre of the old National Aircraft factory at Croydon Airport. The frontage dates from the nineteen-thirties, and was added on to a vintage-First World War structure.

de force, and possibly the finest Art Deco structure in Britain. A complex of several reinforced-concrete buildings, its principal low-lying mass features towers at either end and an outstanding entrance: a huge overdoor sunray-like motif; pilasters with touches of red, black and green; and gates of ornate metalwork. To the left of the factory is the canteen which, with its streamlined elements and central, stepped section, suggests a cinema in its design.

Other London-area industrial structures were the Cox's Building in Watford (Fuller, Hall & Foulsham,. 1937), with a bold central clock tower, and the Sunlight Laundry (F.E. Simpkins, 1936), which featured two bold sunburst reliefs on its façade, these flanking a clock tower over a recessed entryway. Sir Giles Gilbert Scott's Guinness Brewery (1933-36), located in Park Royal, was an asymmetrical complex with handsome brickwork, projecting vertical segments and vertical-fluted bands winding round the tops of each flat-roofed structure. In Southampton, Oliver Bernard's Vickers Supermarine Ltd works (1935-37) was an impressive complex; its office building was a bold five-storey streamlined structure.

A few Moderne factories of note were built in the north of England, in Scotland and in Ireland. The India Tyre and Rubber Factory (Wallis, Gilbert & Partners, 1930-31), Inchinnan, Scotland, was a long, white-washed structure with green, orange and black stripes around the door and entry column. The same firm also designed Burton's factory in Lancashire (1938-39), a mostly red-brick structure with strong black and white tiled elements both vertical and horizontal. In Glasgow, the Leyland Motors Ltd offices and service department (1938) comprised a handsome two-storey brick building centred by a white-stone cylindrical tower with fin-like vertical extensions – which could just as well have adorned an Odeon cinema. The massive black Vitrolite and clear glass wall of the Daily Express Building in Manchester (Sir E. Owen Williams, 1939), through which the rolling presses could be viewed, was similar to its earlier London counterpart in its streamlined-box form. Akin to Wallis, Gilbert's London factories was the Kodak Building in Dublin, an early thirties low-lying, white-sheathed, towered structure.

Lightly ornamented brick buildings predominated among the Moderne factories, warehouses and other industrial buildings constructed in the United States in the nineteen-twenties and thirties. Examples included C. Leslie Weir's various Massachusetts ice company plants, Cubist structures with projecting vertical elements and zigzag bands of brickwork; the light orange brick Pump and Blower Station of the Patapsco Sewage Plant, Baltimore (Frank O. Heyder, 1940), with stepped-in door and window frames and Art Deco lettering on a stainless steel sign; and the Municipal Water Works in Griffin, Georgia, with Streamline scroll-design bas-reliefs over its doors. Somewhat grander was Paul Philippe Cret's Central Heating and Refrigeration Plant in Washington D.C. (1933-34), a brick classical Moderne 'temple of power', its façade set with bas-relief terracotta and limestone panels of mechanical details and machine operators.

In the Art Deco period, factories, warehouses, power stations and other industrial structures were often adorned with decorative elements. Notable production and storage buildings included London's Gillette Factory (*opposite above*), designed by Sir Banister F. Fletcher in 1936; a Hudson Street warehouse in Lower Manhattan (*opposite below left*), its figural bas-reliefs probably by René Paul Chambellan; the nearly symmetrical C.E.I. Power Plant in Ashtabula, Ohio (*opposite below right*); and a striking industrial structure in Dublin (*right*), built as a power-generating house (later incarnations included a Bovril factory, snooker hall and the present-day complex of offices and studios). The original building has been considerably altered by the nineteen-eighties cosmetic addition of gold and black to its façade.

In New York, the sixteen-storey Port of New York Authority Inland Freight Terminal (Abbott, Merkt & Co., c.1932-33) was a stepped mass with the uppermost section crowned by small ziggurat shapes. The same firm created the Hecht Company warehouse in Washington D.C. (1937), whose streamlined façade was made up of alternating horizontal bands of buff-coloured bricks and glass blocks. A geometric pattern of black and white tiles covered the lower façade, and the cylindrical-section corner was topped by a double-decker crown of glass. A notable Philadelphia structure was the Lasher Printing Company (Philip Tyre, 1927), faced with grainy-textured concrete. On parts of the upper section were zigzag and stepped designs in brick, and around the entry was a breezy zigzag pattern and more stepped-brick designs, these punctuated with circles.

A significant working environment was Frank Lloyd Wright's design for S.C. Johnson and Son in Racine, Wisconsin (1936-39), a sprawling array of interconnected administrative and research structures made of brick, glass and translucent plastic tubing. The complex was marked by a multitude of streamlined corners, some ingeniously interlocking, and a lack of right angles; huge support piers shaped like giant golf tees were used both inside and out. Other factories were as defiantly angular as the Johnson Wax buildings were stridently curvilinear. In Toledo, the Owens-Illinois Glass Company was a gleaming glass box, while in Fort Worth, the Dr. Pepper Bottling Company (Hubert Hammond Crane, 1938) was a multi-cubed, white-concrete giant, its tallest segment a stepped bell tower. The asymmetrical, yet subtle decoration and white surface of the plant make it akin to the flat-roofed cubes by Robert Mallet-Stevens, whose buildings managed to be at once Art Deco and Modernist. Similar Cubist structures were the Loma Linda Food Company in Arlington, California (1936-38), a complex of cubes and semicircles with a decided emphasis on the horizontal, and the Bekins Storage Building, Los Angeles (c.1940), a five-storey white concrete and stucco box with three long vertical windows at its front.

Both rectilinear and circular elements made up some of the factories designed by Albert Kahn (1867-1942) of Detroit, the most esteemed designer of American industrial buildings in the nineteen-twenties and thirties (he also worked in the Soviet Union, where his firm designed over 500 factories). His domestic projects included the twenties River Rouge factories of the Ford Motor Company, the Ford Glass Plant in Dearborn (1922) and the Ohio Steel Foundry Roll and Heavy Machine Shop in Lima, Ohio (1938).

On the West Coast, the Coca-Cola Bottling Plant and Office in Los Angeles (1936-37) was a nautical Streamline Moderne palace designed in concrete by Robert V. Derrah, complete with promenade deck, portholes, ship's bridge and other maritime details. The 7-Up Bottling Company Building in Portland, Oregon (Arthur B. Cramer, 1940), was a streamlined white mass with a huge red 7-Up logo atop its entrance tower, a bottle of soda perched atop the sign. The most exotically decorated factory was the

Samson Tyre and Rubber Company (Morgan, Walls & Clements, 1929) in Los Angeles, a neo-Assyrian pile embellished with details drawn from the Nineveh Palace repertoire.

Chicagoan Walter Burley Griffin (1876-1937), who lived in Australia from 1914 until 1935, designed several monumental, partly Mayan Revival structures there, including the City of Sydney Incinerator in Pyrmont and the Willoughby Municipal Incinerator, both with E.M. Nicholls. Among the other notable Australian industrial buildings were the streamlined mass of the Peek Frean (Aust.) Ltd. factory (H.E. Ross & Rowe) and the stepped and curved white-cement boiler house of the Royal Prince Alfred Hospital (Stephenson, Meldrum & Turner), both in Sydney.

Stores and Restaurants

Whether a gleaming highway diner, an attractive shopfront or a huge streamlined department store, Art Deco commercial structures became common sights in thirties America. Except for the retail façade, which could be added to older edifices, such buildings were less common in the Old World. Façades in the style were especially common in Paris, especially on café and brasserie exteriors, many of which were influenced by storefronts and pavilions at the 1925 Exposition. Examples of such Moderne premises were the *chemisier* Covanna in the Rue Pasquier by Pierre Patout, its stucco façade painted with a bold Expressionist pattern, and Louis Süe and André Mare's elegant Parfumerie d'Orsay. René Herbst created stylish shop windows for clients, their names spelled out with smart metal ribbons and straight lines in sans-serif typefaces. The metal components of Henri Sauvage and Frantz Jourdain's Samaritaine department store in the Quai du Louvre (1928) were largely prefabricated; strong Deco elements in the guise of fluted and stepped stone sculptures crowned the upper levels. The same pair's 1926-30 'deco-ization' of Jourdain's earlier Samaritaine, in the Rues de la Monnaie, Baillet et de l'Arbre Sec, was an unnecessary, somewhat unfortunate update of an Art Nouveau showplace.

Two vastly different department stores were built in The Hague. The cooperative store of De Volharding (J.W.E. Buijs & J.B. Lürsen, 1928) was a bold essay in glass and right angles, whereas the face presented by De Bijenkorf (The Beehive), designed by Piet Kramer, was quite antithetical: not only was the 1924-25 store adorned with figural sculptures, there was also a wealth of streamlined, rounded elements on its brick exterior.

Several Art Deco department stores were built in London. Kensington High Street boasted two designed by Bernard George: Derry & Toms (1933) and Barker's (1937-38), the former with ornate figural metalwork grilles and bas-relief panels of stylized blossoms and figures, the latter with two towers of glass and ornament that included reliefs of chic women and spandrels set with leaf forms and store products, including chairs and shoes. Peter Jones (William Crabtree, with Slater & Moberley and C.H. Reilly, 1936-39) struck a more International Style than Moderne note, yet its curved corners and stepped-back, balustraded roof echoed the Coca-Cola Bottling Plant in Los Angeles, and its glass skin was like that of the Daily Express Building.

The Pond's Extract Company (from 1955 Chesebrough-Pond's) factory (*opposite above left*) in Clinton, Connecticut, is an example of an American industrial building with a handsomely designed and maintained façade. The concrete structure was built in 1929 by the Aberthaw Company, considerably expanding what had become the inadequate premises of the highly successful maker of cold and vanishing creams.

One of the largest concentrations of attractive Moderne industrial buildings – in the main, low, white-washed structures – was in suburban London. The finest of these were designed by the firm of Wallis, Gilbert & Partners: their 1932 Hoover Factory (*right*) in Perivale was the undisputed star, but the 1929 Firestone (*opposite right*) in Brentford was a close contender. The entrances of both reinforced-concrete structures featured bold polychrome decoration of an exotic-hybrid style against white-washed grounds with mostly classical features. More rectilinear was Fuller, Hall & Foulsham's 1937 Cox's (later Linpac) Building in Watford (*opposite below left*). Similar to many civic projects of the period, Cox's featured a tall central clock tower. Its palette, however, was very much in the Moderne factory mode.

Industrial Buildings

The London Power Company's mammoth Battersea Power Station (*right*) was designed by Sir Giles Gilbert Scott with engineer S.L. Pearce. In Australia, two slightly later, partly Mayan-inspired, municipal incinerators were designed by Chicagoan Walter Burley Griffin and E.M. Nicholls: the City of Sydney Incinerator at Pyrmont (*opposite above left*) was sheathed with textured synthetic stone, and the Willoughby Municipal Incinerator (*opposite above right*) was a stepped sandstone and concrete building. Both were made by the Reverberatory Incinerator and Engineering Co. Ltd.

The press blurb on the streamlined American Rolling Mill Company laboratory in Middletown, Ohio (*below*), described the 1937 structure as the 'house that research built': in this case from iron, steel, stainless steel and glass bricks. Also in Ohio was the Owens-Illinois Glass Company building in Toledo (*opposite below*), a defiantly angular glass-grid structure of *c.*1936.

Several of the finest Art Deco industrial structures were English: Wallis, Gilbert & Partners' 1929 Firestone Tyre Factory (*left*) – tragically demolished (*above*) on the eve of its becoming a listed property in 1980 – and the 1932 Hoover Factory (*below left*), the design of its canteen (seen at left) akin to that of a streamlined Odeon cinema. Across the Atlantic, Robert V. Derrah's nautically inspired 1936-37 Coca-Cola Building (*bottom*) was one of Los Angeles's most distinctive Streamline Moderne structures, while in Midwestern Detroit the Ford Motor Company's striking Rotunda (*below*) was a dramatic exhibition space that closely resembled a world fair pavilion in the Moderne style.

Ford Rotunda and Administration Building, Dearborn, Mich.

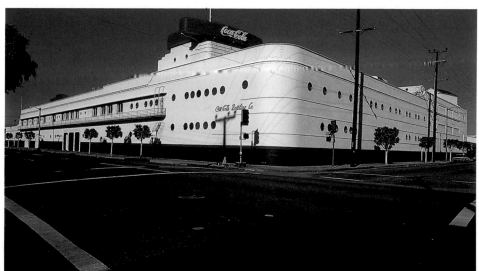

A handsome Gallic-inspired Moderne façade in London's Berkeley Square was that of ladies' clothier Madelon Chaumet (1926). Created by Joseph Emberton, this little storefront, with its Moderne lettering and exuberant ornamental metalwork, was an Art Deco gem. A smart entryway and sign marked the Ford Building in Regent Street (Chas. Heathcote & Sons, c.1930) as well: the company name fronted a sunburst-like design over a wavy base, along whose sides two sleek greyhounds were frozen in motion. On the other hand, E. Maxwell Fry's Westminster Electric Supply Corporation showroom (1934) was as up-to-date as the power it provided, all rounded corners and neon tubes.

Although Tudor- and Georgian-style public houses prevailed in thirties Britain, several Streamline Moderne examples were built, including E.B. Musman's Comet in Hatfield (1936), a two-storey brick structure distinguished by curves and straight lines, stepped sections and bullnoses. Musman's Nag's Head at Bishop's Stortford (c.1935) was a somewhat similar brick structure: even its free-standing sign, perched on a fluted brick column, was Moderne. Oliver Bernard took on Ramsgate brewer Martin Thomson's commission to produce a pub that was 'modern as distinct from imitation period'. The result, the Prospect Inn in Minster-in-Thanet (1938), was a lively assemblage of cubed and rounded elements, including porthole windows and curved, cantilevered overhangs.

Scotland's premier commercial establishment in the Art Deco style was Edinburgh's Maybury Roadhouse (Patterson & Broom, 1936), one of whose sources of inspiration was the ocean liner. Glasgow's streets were enlivened with a mass of Art Deco-style shopfronts, some decorated with zigzags and sunburst motifs, their names spelled out in stylish letters; others with streamlined corners and shiny Vitrolite surfaces. Notable establishments were the Zigzag Moderne Samuel Dow pub-cum-cocktail-bar (Lennox & MacMath and James W. Weddell, 1936-39); the Dominion Restaurant (W.J.B. Wright, 1933), featuring glass panels sandblasted with stars, zigzags and flowerbursts; and Rogano's restaurant (1936), with bold Moderne lettering accompanied by the image of a bright red crayfish. The Glasgow Corporation Gas Department showroom (A. McInnes Gardner, c.1935), with 'GAS' spelled out in bronze relief characters at the top, also featured Parisian-style wave-and-scroll metalwork. C. & A. Modes Ltd. (North, Robin & Wilsdon, 1928-29) was a large Glasgow store which featured faience touches on its rectangular, reinforced-concrete form.

In Dublin, the three-storey Gas Board showroom and offices in D'Olier Street (Robinson & Keefe, 1928) presented a smart Moderne face in dark polished stone, zigzag ornamental grillework, red lettering, chrome detailing and three etched glass windows. In Belfast, architect James Scott gave the Sinclair department store (1926-35) an Art Deco façade of cream-coloured faience tiles.

New York had the lion's share of stores and restaurants in various Art Deco modes. Major firms included Bloomingdale's, to which a quasi-Mayan Revival extension by Starrett & Van Vleck was added in 1930, and the S.H.

The shape of this *c*.1937 Hollywood haberdashers is undeniably Streamline Moderne, but its cladding was more in the high-style Parisian vein. It was designed by Douglas Honnold.

Kress & Co. Building (Edward Sibbert, 1935), comprising a '5, 10, 25 cent store' and offices with decoration inspired by Pre-Columbian sources; like Barker's in London, Kress 'advertised' some of its wares in the guise of square-section relief panels on its façade. Two exclusive Fifth Avenue establishments were elegant boxes with Moderne touches: some 80 per cent of the two street-facing sides of Steuben Glass's five-storey showroom (William & Geoffrey Platt and John M. Gates, 1937) were glass blocks, with handsome relief panels just under the flat-roof line, and Tiffany's (Cross & Cross, 1939-40) was essentially Neoclassical, with a faint Art Deco reference in its overdoor clock, carried on the back of a nude male figure. One of the showiest retail stores in Manhattan was Stewart & Company (Warren & Wetmore, 1928-29), whose dramatic front entrance was altered by Ely Jacques Kahn a mere eight months later in 1930, when Bonwit Teller took over the building.

The wrought-iron and gilt-bronze front door of the Cheney Brothers silk store in Fifth Avenue was an authentic French component, created by Ferrobrandt, the New York branch of Parisian *ferronnier* Edgar Brandt; it was composed of stylized blossoms and leaves topped by a golden fountain motif. Other notable French-inspired storefronts included that of the perfumer Delettrez (John Frederick Coman, *c*.1927); the Wise Shoe Shop (Elias Rothschild & Co., *c*.1928); and Nat Lewis (S.S. Silver & Co., *c*.1928). In a category of its own was Joseph Urban's Bedell department store (1926), its façade a smart surface of zigzag and stepped elements, polished stone and ornate metalwork.

Several Art Deco building types were represented in the Horn & Hardart Automat cafeterias which sprang up in New York and Philadelphia in the thirties (the first Automat opened in Philadelphia in 1902). One of the finest was in 181st Street, New York (Louis Allen Abramson, 1930-31), and it featured a polychrome zigzag ribbon on the cornice, a band of stylized blossoms and sunbursts below that and handsome metal light fixtures. Near Pennsylvania Station on 34th Street was a contemporaneous Abramson design, this with four pilasters topped by stylized male figures (their inspiration supposedly Josef Hoffmann's Palais Stoclet in Brussels), as well as elements from the standard floral, geometric and scroll repertoire. The 57th Street Automat (Ralph B. Bencker, 1938) was a hearty evocation of the buff terracotta-faced Odeon-Streamline Moderne School.

This latter façade type appeared profusely throughout the country, on shops, restaurants and cafes, but notably on that ubiquitous retail establishment, the 'five and dime', whether of the H.L. Green, Kresge, J.J. Newberry or Woolworth variety, to name but a few. As in Britain, sleek Vitrolite, often combined with glass bricks, was a popular material for American storefronts, and it was employed in both the ornate zigzag and toned-down streamline modes. New or improved metals and alloys in various combinations were a handsome alternative as well. For example, Desco (Detroit Show Case Co.) copper, bronze and aluminium alloy storefronts were advertised as improvements to existing premises.

Paris in the nineteen-twenties was rich in Moderne storefronts, their ornamental metalwork, stylish lettering, and geometric and floral embellishments evoking pavilions at the 1925 Exposition. Typical were the Boulevard des Capucines premises of the hairdresser-perfumer Girault (*above left*), by architects Azema, Edrei & Hardy, and Pierre Patout's stucco-sheathed Covanna shop in the Rue Pasquier (*left*), its lower façade enhanced with a bold Expressionist pattern. Its Gallic name and appearance notwithstanding, the Madelon Chaumet ladies' clothing shop (*above*) was in London's Berkeley Square; it was designed by Joseph Emberton in 1926 immediately after the Paris fair (though by the late nineteen-forties it was gone).

Many American retail establishments were designed in *le style moderne*; the owners of such shops as Burdine's of Miami Beach (*below*) were eager to be associated with French style. Gallic-inspired motifs filtered down to the most ordinary retail stores, largely in the guise of polychrome terracotta panels that could be purchased from various suppliers. A fine example of such 'generic Deco' ornament is the tiling on McKecknie & Trask's *c.*1929 Kansas City retail store (*above*).

Outstanding Moderne decoration surrounded the entrance of Warren & Wetmore's 1928-29 Stewart and Company on New York's Fifth Avenue, in the form of Trygve Hammer's short-lived metal and faience frieze depicting the fountains of youth and beauty (less than a year later it was replaced by Ely Jacques Kahn's geometric design for new owner Bonwit Teller). This building was demolished in 1980 to make way for the Trump Tower.

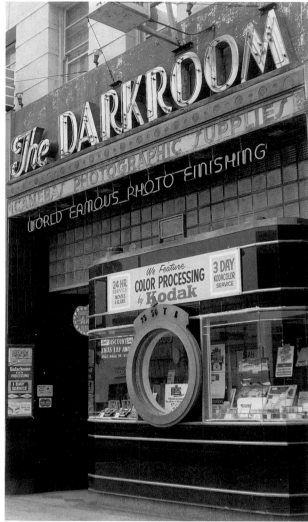

From popular neon-lit cafés in Paris to Streamline Moderne drive-in eateries around Hollywood, commercial establishments in the Moderne vein made myriad and diverse appearances. In the French capital were La Coupole (*opposite above*), in Montparnasse, the Idéale 'biscuiterie' (*opposite below right*), and the 1928 Cafés du Brésil (*above right*). In southern California, where the automobile was rapidly increasing in numbers, fast-food drive-ins were all the rage by the thirties. These often featured an arresting vertical motif-cum-sign: like Carpenter's in Hollywood (*opposite below left*) and the Rall's 'drive-in station' (*right*), surmounted by a Moderne teapot. Most of the window façade of the 1938 Los Angeles photographic-supplies store, the Darkroom, was an advertising gimmick – black Vitrolite and silvered metal in the guise of a camera; it was designed by Marcus P. Miller.

That uniquely American eating establishment, the diner, could be found up and down the Northeast from the nineteen-thirties (even in the post-war years, the basic diner design remained that of the earlier models). In Middletown, Connecticut, O'Rourke's Diner (*opposite below*) was built by Mountain View of New Jersey in the forties. Philadelphia's Oak Lane Diner (*opposite above*) is a large gleaming eatery punctuated with coloured stripes. Albuquerque's 66 Diner (*left*) is a world apart from the classic East Coast eatery but is nonetheless a fine example of Streamline Moderne. On the other side of the Atlantic, the 1936 Maybury Roadhouse in Edinburgh (*above*) was a stylish British diner, whose façade was once appropriately compared to a Rolls-Royce radiator grille. Designed by Patterson & Broom in 1936, it is now a restaurant and conference centre, and one of Scotland's finest Art Deco buildings.

Los Angeles was home to several large Art Deco department stores. Bullock's Wilshire (*opposite left*) was directly inspired by the 1925 Paris Exposition, which the co-founder of the store, P.G. Winnett, had visited; today I. Magnìn, it was designed by John Parkinson and Donald B. Parkinson in 1929. In the Streamline Moderne vein were Coulter's (*left*), designed by Stiles O. Clements in 1937 (and demolished in 1980), and the 1940 May Co. (*below*), by Albert Martin and S.A. Marx.

The Rex Cole showroom in Brooklyn (*above*) was designed by Raymond M. Hood in 1931. The top step of the setback structure was a giant General Electric icebox, of the type that was sold within by the appliance distributor.

The black and gold terracotta sheathing the 1929 Security First National Bank of Los Angeles (now Security Pacific Bank) Building (*right*) is similar to that on the old Atlantic Richfield Building (no longer extant); both were designed by Morgan, Walls & Clements.

The Gas Board showroom and offices in D'Olier Street, Dublin (*opposite*), present an attractive Moderne face. Unfortunately, the upper-storey windows no longer have their original zigzag grillework, but the three etched glass windows remain. The polished-stone building was designed by Robinson & Keefe in 1928.

Vitrolite, that versatile vitreous material, was used extensively on shop and bar fronts in the Art Deco period. Often it was enhanced by lively lettering, as on the Rogano Restaurant and Fish Bar in Glasgow (*below right*), redesigned by A. McEwan & Co. in 1936: in other instances, its vivid colouring was decoration enough, as on Crawford's Restaurant and Cafeteria (*below*) in Camden, New Jersey.

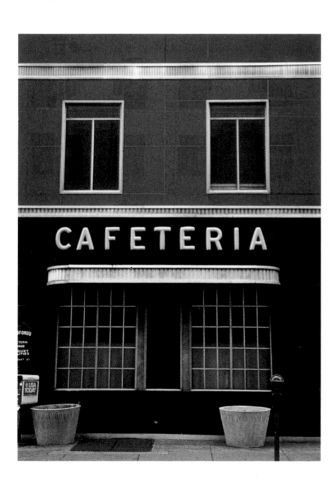

Many motifs were on offer, including a wide array of sunbursts, zigzags and stepped sections in the range of fronts. Even marble was used to give old stores new Moderne façades: Vermont Marble's series of 'Modernistic Movement' advertisements spotlighted the Baker Shoe Store in Hollywood (Myron Hunt & H.C. Chambers, c.1930), with its lavish use of Belgian black and white Vermont marble in the Moderne vein, and the Stark Marble & Tile showroom in Canton, Ohio (Firestone & Christman, c.1932), its sides faux-pilasters topped with stylized-wing capitals.

In 1931, two tour-de-force showrooms were designed in New York by Raymond Hood for Rex Cole Inc., a distributor of General Electric refrigerators. In Flushing, Queens, he created a huge white cube, topped with a cylindrical penthouse mimicking the compressor on actual GE iceboxes. In Brooklyn a stepped stone structure with a glass extension bore the firm's name in Moderne lettering on the central cube, which was surmounted by a giant GE refrigerator.

The no-nonsense eatery known as the diner began to dot the roadways of the eastern United States in the thirties (there were even some in big cities, like the Empire and Cheyenne in Manhattan and the Oak Lane in Philadelphia). Its primary building materials were glass bricks and stainless steel, chrome or aluminium, with larger segments of metal often stamped with relief sunburst or zigzag patterns; touches of colour were provided by horizontal or vertical stripes (painted or glazed) and neon signs. Most authentic thirties to fifties diners — which were prefabricated in factories — had long, streamlined forms derived from industrial designs and were meant to resemble a trolley or railroad car. Some unusually shaped ones were built, however, like the 1937 White Manna in Hackensack, New Jersey, a sixteen-foot-wide square with curved sides. These gleaming eateries proliferated in their birthplace, the Northeast, and they ranged southwards to the Mid-Atlantic states; occasional Midwestern and Western examples were also to be found. The first American fast-food chain, White Tower, which began in 1926, was a countrywide fixture. By the thirties White Tower's standard white-sheathed, single-turreted form appeared in Deco-style variants, enhanced with glass blocks, Vitrolite, Moderne lettering and stainless steel and coloured terracotta highlights; most had curved corners, but some were starkly rectilinear. Many White Towers were created by Charles J. Johnson, the company's in-house architect. In similar style, laundries and dry-cleaners proliferated all over the United States.

In Miami Beach, several commercial buildings deserve mention. The old Hoffman's Cafeteria (Henry Hohauser, 1939) includes strong cylindrical and circular elements, and a profusion of glass brick. The former Friedman's Bakery, awash with fluted, zigzag and scrolled elements — and dominated by an octagonal stepped turret at its corner — was one of the town's most-photographed buildings in the early nineteen-eighties, when it was a pastel-painted confection appropriate to its function. In Miami proper the massive c.1929 Sears Roebuck building is a grand towering structure, and the single stepped mass of Burdine's Boulevard Shop, with its Gallic-style,

With its Native American-derived motifs and palette, the Pueblo Deco style informed a wealth of buildings in the American West and Southwest. A detail from the white terracotta-clad Skinner building, a 1931 Albuquerque grocery store, is illustrated here (below), while the aluminium fan motif (opposite) adorns Wright's Trading Post, c.1935, in the same New Mexico city.

stylized-floral overdoor decoration, would not have been out of place in New York or Paris.

Pueblo Deco commercial buildings can be found in New Mexico, Arizona and Texas. In Albuquerque, Maisel's Trading Post (John Gaw Meem, 1937) was distinguished for its zigzag aluminium grillework, terrazzo entry floor (decorated with a thunderbird of inlaid coral and turquoise) and mural, which depicted events from Apache, Navajo and Pueblo life painted by Native American artists. Wright's Trading Post (c.1935), also in Albuquerque, includes fluted, fan and stepped-diamond decoration, and several grid patterns of turquoise opalescent glass tiles (meant to entice customers to buy the turquoise jewellery on sale; they were also a Hopi symbol for stacked ears of blue corn). The Skinner Building in Albuquerque was a grocery store designed by A.W. Boehning in 1931; it displayed a wealth of Moderne motifs, including stylized volutes, zigzags and wavy bands, some of which were part of the Native American design vocabulary. In Amarillo, Texas, the buff brick-clad White & Kirk Building (Guy Carlander, 1938) mixed indigenous flora motifs (the yucca cactus) with Art Deco zigzags on a terracotta band above the department store's first storey. Also in Amarillo, another Pueblo Deco store was S.H. Kress (Edward Sibbert, 1932), a stepped, buff-brick building set with standard-issue polychrome floral terracotta panels near the top.

Los Angeles's major retail building of the period was Bullock's Wilshire (now I. Magnin) store (John and Donald B. Parkinson, 1929), a stepped, towering pile of tan terracotta with copper detailing. Much of its design inspiration came from France: cofounder P.G. Winnett had visited the 1925 Exposition and afterwards wanted his store designed in *le style moderne*. Many motifs were Gallic in taste, such as the ornamental metalwork, but other elements were strongly American, like Herman Sachs's massive ceiling fresco, 'Speed of Transportation', in the motor court: its centrepiece was a turquoise Mercury set amid an ocean liner, dirigible, locomotive and aeroplanes. Another deluxe Deco building was the Selig Retail Store (Arthur E. Harvey, 1931), which featured a wealth of glazed gold and black terracotta tiling at its upper level. Two massive corner-curved-box department stores were May Co. (Albert Martin & S.A. Marx, 1940) and Coulter's (Stiles O. Clements, 1937).

More downmarket, but no less interesting, retail establishments – including drive-in restaurants – began to carpet the southern Californian landscape in the twenties and thirties. The Darkroom (1938) was a camera store whose façade was a giant Vitrolite and metal camera, and the Crossroads of the World shopping centre in Hollywood (Robert V. Derrah, 1936) had a nautical theme akin to the same architect's Coca-Bottling Plant. Ralph's Supermarket in Inglewood (Stiles O. Clements, 1940), one of many the architect designed for the chain, was an undistinguished, flat-roofed white mass, except for the bold perpendicular slab of a sign that towered overhead.

Department stores in both vertical and horizontal modes were built throughout Europe in various contemporary styles. Two antithetical structures were constructed in The Hague: the 1924-25 De Bijenkorf (The Beehive) (*opposite*), by Amsterdam School architect Piet Kramer, and the cooperative De Volharding (*above right*), by J.W.E. Buijs and J.B. Lürsen. A pair of side-stepped glass turrets dominated Barker's (*above*) in Kensington High Street, London, built in 1937-38. Frankfurt's Römerstadt shopping centre (*right*), by municipal architect Ernst May, was a curving nautical-Moderne affair, complete with porthole windows and upper-level 'deck'.

That initially Californian phenomenon, the fast-food drive-in restaurant, also tended to feature a bold upwards-pointing sign. Carpenter's Drive-In in Hollywood (1935) looked like a giant stylized fountain, while Herbert's (c.1938) was more like a stationary top.

Along the commercial streets of Napier, New Zealand, are a wealth of stylish Moderne storefronts. Among them are the Hawke's Bay Chambers, Masson House (E.A. Williams, 1931) and Kidsons Building, originally the Smith and Chambers Building (H. Alfred Hill, 1932). In Australia, some of the most charming Art Deco structures were the milk bars that thrived in the thirties. Their coloured glass and shiny metal elements, as on the pale green glazed McGovern's Milk Bar in Perth, were reminiscent of the decoration of American diners. In Melbourne there were numerous Depression-era dairies which had Moderne aspects, including futuristic-like fins attached to simple structures. Buckley and Nunn's, a Melbourne department store, featured decorative panels of sunbursts and other conventionalized motifs, these produced by the Wunderlich firm of Sydney, which specialized in architectural terracotta and ornamental metalwork in the Art Deco style.

Cinemas and Theatres

The hugely popular 'palace of entertainment', the cinema, was possibly *the* universal Art Deco structure. Whether in New York, Paris, Buenos Aires or Madras they featured a stream of black-and-white moving images from Hollywood and elsewhere behind their generally attractive, inviting façades. Just as Hollywood films played Peoria as well as Paris and Perth in the Art Deco period, so purpose-built cinemas acquired a readily recognized, exuberantly made-up face – in general, lavish in the twenties, streamlined in the thirties. There were regional and national variations, like the buff-tiled British Odeon, the Mayan Revival cinema of the American West and the largely North American outdoor drive-in, but during the Golden Age of Hollywood the norm was for a picture palace to have as much personality outside as celluloid stars inside.

But people did not only go to films for entertainment. They went to the theatre, dance halls, swimming pools, zoos, amusement parks, museums, casinos and live musical concerts, the latter held outdoors as well as in huge auditoriums, which often doubled as civic structures (for political conventions and the like). They visited the international expositions so prevalent during the period and they also belonged to private (sometimes exclusive or secret) clubs or societies. Structures related to all these activities were designed in the Art Deco style.

In Europe, cinemas and theatres both exotic and streamlined were built. Among the former were the lavish Tuschinski Theater in Amsterdam (1918-21), its façade punctuated with ornate Expressionist motifs, and the Paris Gaumont (1931), a fountain-like form over its entrance. The earlier Théâtre des Champs-Elysées in Paris (Auguste Perret, 1913-14) was a flat-roofed, largely Neoclassical pile, but its allegorical bas-reliefs by Antoine Bourdelle looked forward to panels on Art Deco cinemas, such as those on New York's Radio City Music Hall and London's Warner Leicester Square (E.A. Stone &

The nineteen-thirties Marble Arch Regal became an Odeon in the nineteen-fifties; its tower resembles that of the present-day Leicester Square Odeon; it was demolished in 1964.

T. Somerford, 1938). An exuberant, sensuous figure appeared on the façade of the Folies-Bergère, in the form of a huge bas-relief of a sleek, stylish dancer by Picot. In Germany, Poland and other eastern European countries cinemas and theatres were on the whole less decorative, but some contained Moderne elements. Hans Poelzig's Capitol cinema in Berlin (1925), for instance, presented a straightforward double-columned façade, but its title sign and marquee were enlivened with four-sided stars superimposed on stylized suns. The Kino Gdynia in Łódź, Poland, had a simple arched form flanked by turrets, but on its upper balcony was stylized-wave metalwork from the Parisian design repertoire.

In North Africa, the French influence was evident on the smart Palmarium cinema in Tunis and the theatre in Sidi bel Abbes, Algeria. The Casino cinema in Madras, on the other hand, as well as the Rex in Kuching, Sarawak, bore a resemblance to British Odeons, with their stepped forms and prominent vertical elements in the centre.

Britain's Astorias, Carltons, Odeons, Regents and numerous other thirties cinemas were among the world's finest picture palaces. Filmgoing was the most popular leisure activity in Britain at that time, so owners had every reason to make their cinemas attractive and alluring to audiences, not only by showing films the public wanted to see, but by giving their premises an inviting, and easily identifiable, look.

Oscar Deutsch, a onetime scrap-metal merchant, was the premier champion of the 'brand image' cinema. The first Odeons were launched in 1933, and they well illustrated Deutsch's innovative concept of building cinemas in a like, recognizable style. Deutsch's dream was initially made a reality by Birmingham architects Harry Weedon and Cecil Clavering, with George Coles, Andrew Mather and Robert Bullivant later joining the design team. The Odeon's 'house style' was essentially marked by the use of cream-coloured faience tiles, streamlined curves, finned towers and other extensions, and clean, crisp lines. Among the outstanding Odeons were those in Weston-super-Mare (1935), Clacton (1936), Sutton Coldfield (1936), Muswell Hill (1936), Leicester Square (1937), Woolwich (1937), Balham (1938), Merton (1938) and Middlesbrough (1939).

Other Deco cinemas of note in Britain were the Carlton in Essex Road, London (George Coles, 1930), a polychrome-tinged Egyptian Revival fantasy; Verity & Beverley's Paramount Theatre/Cinema in Birmingham (1937), a wealth of streamlined neon on its vertical sign and under its awning; and the Grosvenor (later Odeon) Cinema in Rayners Lane, Harrow (F.E. Bromige, 1935), its concave-curved, glazed central section punctuated with a huge cabriole-leg-like projection. Margate's Dreamland (Iles, Leathart & Granger, 1934) was an entertainment centre combining cinema, ballroom, restaurant and amusement park; it was somewhat akin to an Odeon, only with a red brick and glass block façade.

A handsome Liverpool auditorium was the Philharmonic Hall (Herbert J. Rowse, 1933), its strong brick silhouette featuring two bullnose sides, a stepped rectangular centre and abstract geometric forms over simple Cubist piers. The Saville Theatre in Shaftesbury Avenue, London (T.P. Bennett & Partners, 1932), was a patterned brick box with an elaborate frieze at the second-storey level and other relief elements.

Notable Scottish cinemas were the Embassy, Glasgow (James McKissack, 1936), its symmetrical mass including two Moderne towers decorated with creamy faience tiles; Govan's Vogue (James McKissack, 1937), also with a faience-covered front, this a fluted and stepped convex curve protruding from a brick back; and the Streamline Moderne Ascot (Charles J. McNair, 1940), its cream-tiled front framed by two bullnoses and highlighted with touches of black and red faience tiles. Dance halls, similar in design to cinemas, were popular Scottish entertainment palaces, a handsome example being the Dennistoun Palais de Danse (Charles J. McNair, 1938).

In Ireland, Michael Scott's nautical-Moderne Ritz Cinema, in Athlone, County Meath (1938-39), was unusually progressive. The Theatre Royal (now demolished, but once the country's largest cinema) and the adjacent Regal in Dublin, both from 1934-35 and by Leslie Norton, with Michael Scott and Norman Good, were lively Moderne essays, the Royal with stylized masks on the cornice, the Regal with jazzy figural panels. The Dublin firm of Robinson & Keefe was probably the foremost Irish exponent of the Art Deco style, and their related cinema designs included the Gaiety in Sligo, the Savoy in Waterford and the Carlton in Dublin (1935-37), which recalled the neo-Egyptian Carlton in London, but without the colour.

A superb South American Art Deco cinema was the Plaza in Buenos Aires, its façade a stepped mass of five glazed, Cubist towers, its low entrance surmounted by jazzy letters. The Teatro Nacional in Santiago, Chile, purpose-built in the late twenties for sound films, was a handsome structure with zigzag, fluted and stepped elements.

Australia boasted a wide range of cinema types, from Walter Burley Griffin's Capitol Theatre in Melbourne (1924), integrated with a ten-storey office building and featuring a wealth of Mayan Revival-by-way-of-Frank-Lloyd Wright abstract geometric designs, to the open-air Roxy Gardens (1935) in Leeton, New South Wales, mostly Spanish-style but with some Moderne stepped and rayed elements. Also in Sydney were Charles Bohringer's Embassy (1934), with a huge classical-Moderne relief over the entrance and stepped door frames; the same architect's St James' Theatre, its entrance enhanced with an array of fluted, scrolled and zigzag designs of Monel metal; and C. Bruce Dellit's Liberty Theatre (1934), a superb Streamline Moderne cinema of stepped section, with a bold two-sided vertical sign. A similar ziggurat façade with fin-like protruding vertical sign decorated the Plaza Theatre, Perth (W.G. Bennett, with H. Vivian Taylor & Soilleux, 1938), while the streamlined, boxy Ozone in Mildura, Victoria (H. Vivian Taylor & Soilleux) featured a pair of vertical signs attached to bullnose sides.

In North America, the local movie house was for many citizens the only Art Deco structure with which they were intimately familiar, with the average working man and woman finding a welcome escape and release in the comfortable, often opulent surroundings of the local Palace, Hollywood, Capitol or Paramount. Many American cinemas and theatres, especially in the twenties, were designed in exotic, revival styles. Cinemas inspired by Pre-Columbian sources began to appear considerably earlier, such as the Aztec Theater in Eagle Pass, Texas (Leonard F. Seed, 1915). Later examples could be strictly Mayan-influenced, with barely a Moderne touch, such as the densely surface-decorated Mayan Theater in Los Angeles (Morgan, Walls & Clements, 1927), a mix of Mayan and Aztec elements, or they could be hybrid beasts, like the Mayan Theater in Denver (Montana Fallis, 1930), with its stepped form, zigzag bands, vertical sign and dominant bas-relief of a Mayan warrior. Elsewhere in the Southwest, cinemas with Native American motifs were built, such as the KiMo Theater in Albuquerque (Robert & Carl Boller, 1927), converted from a legitimate theatre into a cinema in the nineteen-thirties. The Pueblo Deco KiMo was faced with stucco (to imitate adobe) and then adorned with a wealth of polychrome terracotta designs, all derived from Native American sources but with some familiar components of the Art Deco vocabulary.

In California above all, exterior cinema design — not just the flat façade, but the overall shape — often added up to a glittering display: some parts might derive from 1925 Paris, others from a D.W. Griffith epic, still others from sources like ancient Greece and the Far East. Two Los Angeles cinemas, the Wiltern Theater (S. Charles Lee, 1929-31) and the Pantages Theater (B. Marcus Priteca, 1929-30), featured ornate exteriors with a heavy mix of high-style Parisian motifs. Lee, a prominent cinema designer, adapted his flamboyant style to the less opulent Streamline Moderne taste of the thirties, his Academy Theatre in Inglewood (1939) a glass-brick, rounded pile with a towering, fluted-chimney-stack of a sign, wrapped all round with a snaking spiral and topped with a three-dimensional sunburst.

A superb cinema in Oakland was designed by the San Francisco-based architect Timothy L. Pflueger. The Paramount (1931) boasted perhaps the most lavish, certainly the largest, Art Deco figural image on its façade, a mosaic of two puppeteers divided by a vertical sign.

An important cinema designer in the United States was Austrian-born, New York-based John Eberson, who created the Rex in Paris in 1932 with Auguste Bluysen. In the Washington, D.C., area he designed the Penn (1935) and Beverly (1938), both dominated by Streamline Moderne marquees, while the Silver (1938), in Silver Spring, Maryland, sported a smart vertical sign of a nautical bent (a theme running through the Eberson-designed shopping centre in which the cinema was located). His Highland Theatre (1940) featured a Vitrolite-framed entrance and, over this, a pattern of tan and black bricks imitating sprocket holes on film. Another handsome Washington cinema was the Trans-Lux (Thomas Lamb, 1936), whose marquee was surmounted by a prismatic glass tower; the theatre was part of a cinema-retail-office complex that had been likened to an ocean liner with its long, sweeping lines and projecting verticals.

147

More than any other types of building in the nineteen-twenties and especially the thirties, cinemas (and to a lesser extent legitimate theatres), came to define – and glamorize – modern architecture. The cinema was perhaps the only truly international, pancultural Art Deco building, as the geographic range of examples on these (and some of the following) pages show. Seen here are the Plaza in Buenos Aires (*opposite left*), London's 1931 Troxy (later the London Opera Centre) by George Coles (*opposite above right*), the Lido cinema in Venice (*left*), the theatre in Sidi bel Abbes, Algeria (*opposite below right*) and the Folies-Bergère in Paris (*above*), featuring Picot's exuberant bas-relief of a dancer.

American picture palaces ranged from huge exotic confections inspired by Mayan, Aztec, Egyptian and Greek architecture, to sleek Streamline Moderne structures. Virtually all made use of strands of neon lighting, sometimes simply to announce their name over the

marquee, but in other instances, as on the 1937 Bruin Theatre in Los Angeles (*opposite below*), to create elaborate neon sculptures. Smart Moderne lettering – both vertical and horizontal – distinguishes the stepped façade of the Drexel in Columbus, Ohio (*opposite above*); it was

designed and built in 1937 by Robert R. Royce. Miami Beach's Cameo (*above*) features, over a large window of glass bricks, a large carved keystone relief panel, its subject a cameo in a surround of stylized blossoms and palm fronds. The architect of this 1936 cinema was Robert E. Collins.

The salient feature of many cinemas the world over was a vertical element: a towering pylon, parapet or other latter-day obelisk that stood out like a lighthouse's beacon. Britain's Odeons were especially notable for such embellishments, as exhibited by two cream-coloured, faience-clad designs by Georges Coles, the 1937 Odeon Woolwich (*above right*) and the 1938 Odeon Balham (*left*). Even as far afield as Kuching, in Sarawak, Indonesia, the Rex (*above left*) followed a similar architectural formula. Doubtless S. Charles Lee's Academy in Inglewood (*opposite*) was one of the Los Angeles area's tallest cinemas: its main area comprised interlocking stucco-clad cylinders, but its crowning glory was a 125-feet-high fluted-chimney-stack sign, wrapped all around with a snaking spiral (that was originally lit with blue neon) and surmounted by a three-dimensional sun.

153

From small-town to big-city America, cinemas were built in earnest to accommodate the record numbers of moviegoers in the twenties and thirties. Some were discreetly integrated into their urban contexts, as Boak & Paris's 1933 Metro (*above*), on Manhattan's upper Broadway, its façade decorated with a roundel depicting Comedy and Tragedy. Altogether more cinematic and dramatic – and of the soaring vertical-extension genre – are A. Hurley Robinson's Curzon Loughborough of 1936 (*right*) and, near San Francisco, A.A. Cantin's 1941 Orinda (*opposite right*), its massive piers like those on several exhibits at the 1939 Golden Gate Exposition (see page 53).

John J, Zink, of the Baltimore firm Zink, Atkins & Crawford, was a prolific cinema designer, with numerous commissions in Washington, Maryland and New York. The Uptown Theater in Washington (1936) was a stepped, symmetrical structure with a subtle zigzag ribbon under its horizontal sign and a wealth of relief bands. Zink's 1939 Senator cinema in Baltimore was another handsome essay in symmetry and taste; glass brick, Bakelite, stainless steel and neon were among the new materials used both inside and out.

The Pickwick Theatre in Park Ridge, Illinois (R. Harold Zook, c.1931), was one of the Midwest's finest cinemas, the façade of its central stepped mass set with a huge stylized sunburst over a recessed arch. Two other notable cinemas were the Fox Detroit Theater and the Paramount, Aurora, Illinois.

In tropical Miami Beach, several Art Deco cinemas were built to complement the area's Moderne hotels and apartments. The Cameo Theatre (Robert E. Collins, 1936) featured a huge carved-keystone panel: on it an oval cameo portrait of a woman was set amid a sea of stylized blossoms and palm fronds; other design elements of the Cameo were of the Streamline Moderne variety. Collins also designed the Lincoln Theatre (1935-36), again with a rectangular panel as a parapet.

Two Pennsylvania cinemas deserve mention. In Norristown, the Norris Theatre (William H. Lee, 1930) was a terracotta-sheathed, gilded palace of grand design (but relatively modest proportions). Over the marquee a scroll-ended, fountain-like motif framed by two fluted pilasters was fashioned of green and gold terracotta, while the stepped crest featured a gilded zigzag ribbon topped by a band of fluted verticals; a bold vertical sign extended over the roof line. Philadelphia's Mayfair Theater (David Supowitz, 1936) was a significant Streamline Moderne exercise in its use of horizontal bands, curved marquee and new materials.

New York's Art Deco cinemas echoed various sources — Mayan, Greek and Egyptian among them — but the bulk were thoroughly Moderne (legitimate theatres were generally more traditional). Radio City Music Hall, part of the Rockefeller Center complex, was tastefully decorated on its exterior with three oval bas-reliefs by Hildreth Meiere; the polychrome medallions held ornate, if sombre, allegorical figures of Song, Drama and Dance. A similar relief roundel dominated the façade of the Midtown cinema on upper Broadway (Boak & Paris, 1933). Joseph Urban created several New York theatres; these are not considered Art Deco, but their designs had a bearing on those that are. The Ziegfeld Theater (1926-27) was praised for its proscenium-like stone façade, decorated with zigzag bands, huge urns and monumental figures. On the other hand, the Max Reinhardt Theater (1929) showed Urban's Viennese roots with its gridwork elements, but also contained stepped Moderne segments.

Massive auditoriums and coliseums were related to cinemas and theatres, though their scale usually precluded lavish use of ornament. Possibly the finest Streamline Moderne auditorium was the Pan-Pacific in Los Angeles (Walter Wurdeman & Welton Becket, 1935). Its towering glory was the

Leisure Buildings

quartet of fin-like, aerodynamic flagpole pylons at its entry, which resembled the industrial design-influenced elements on pavilions at the Chicago Century of Progress exhibition. On the other hand, the Will Rogers Memorial Complex in Fort Worth, Texas (Herman P. Koeppe for Wyatt C. Hedrick, 1936) was a unified, harmonious Pueblo Deco complex comprising coliseum, auditorium and tower. A more classical-Moderne note was sounded in Chautauqua, New York, in the Norton Memorial Hall (Otis F. Johnson, c.1930-31), a light-hued mass of reinforced concrete whose corner pylons were set with bas-relief figural panels by Fred M. Torry.

Outdoor concert 'bowls' were Moderne by virtue of their shape, the stepped-back arches of their hemispherical forms resembling a giant sunburst. Especially attractive was the orchestral shell in Grant Park, Chicago (E.V. Buchsbaum, c.1932), as well as the Napier, New Zealand, Sound Shell (J.T. Watson). Outdoor playing fields and stadiums, too, were designed with Moderne elements, such as Farrington Field in Fort Worth (Preston M. Geren, Sen., 1939), with strong Neoclassical overtones, and the Shawfield greyhound racing stadium in Glasgow (John Easton, 1936), whose entranceway featured a pair of Art Deco wrought-iron lamps atop pilasters and a gate with scrolled and zigzag bands.

Two observatories in the Moderne style were Chicago's Adler Planetarium (Ernest Grunsfeld, 1930) and Los Angeles' Griffith Observatory (John C. Austin & Frederick M. Ashley, 1935). Several museums, too, featured Art Deco elements, including the Panhandle Plains Museum in Canyon, Texas (E.F. Rittenberry, 1932), a Pueblo Deco structure with stylized limestone bas-reliefs of cowboys, Indians, eagles and native flora mixed in with zigzag and wavy bands. Bebb & Gould's Seattle Art Museum (1933) was a classical-monumental structure, but the shiny metal grillework above its entryway was Art Deco. The Castlemaine Art Museum and Gallery in Victoria, Australia, is housed in a 1932 Art Deco building.

Amusement parks, zoos and other outdoor entertainment complexes in the United States, Britain and Australia often incorporated Art Deco elements in their design (one of their foremost precursors was Frank Lloyd Wright's 1914 Midway Gardens in Chicago). Pavilions of the Glen Echo (Maryland) Amusement Park (Alexander, Becker & Schoeppe, 1931-39) included Streamline Moderne elements, as did Lakeside Park in Denver, Luna Park in Sydney and other thirties parks. Denver's Picnic Pavilion in Elitch Gardens featured a stepped tower dotted with sunburst and chevron motifs, and even the Thomas Jefferson Memorial Building, the entrance to Virginia's Grand Caverns, was Moderne in aspect, its dramatic overdoor parapet black and stepped. Brooklyn's Coney Island included notable Art Deco structures, such as Walker & Gillette's music tower in Playland, as did Jones Beach, Long Island, with its turreted bath houses (W. Earle Andrews & Herbert A. Magoon, c.1931-32). Britain's Modernist/International Style seaside complex, the De La Warr Pavilion at Bexhill (Erich Mendelsohn & Serge Chermayeff, 1933-36), presented a different kind of face to the 'architecture of pleasure'.

Cinemas, Theatres and Leisure Buildings

The exotic cinema, its sources ranging from Meso-American ziggurats to Egyptian pylons, appeared more in the nineteen-twenties than the thirties, the latter being the age of the Streamline Moderne movie theatre. A quartet of classically inspired cinemas are illustrated here: the 1927 Mayan Theater in Los Angeles (*below*), by Morgan, Walls & Clements, a densely decorated visual medley of Mayan and Aztec motifs; George Coles's 1930 Egyptian Revival Carlton (*right*) in Essex Road, London, now a bingo hall; the 1927 KiMo Theater in Albuquerque (*right below*), Italian immigrant Oreste Bachechi's tribute to the American Southwest designed by Robert and Carl Boller (its façade is polychrome terracotta-studded stucco, but made to resemble Pueblo adobe); and Miller & Pflueger's magnificent 1931 Oakland Paramount (*opposite right*), with its Neoclassical tile mural (today it is home to the Oakland Symphony Orchestra).

The rectilinear Moderne cinema and theatre, with hardly a curve on its angular exterior, was another international type; its design was in part indebted to Willem Marinus Dudok's Hilversum Town Hall in the Netherlands, in part to the nascent International Style. The Regal Uxbridge (*opposite above*) was designed by E. Norman Bailey in 1931 and included the zigzag motif on its façade; a similar boxy form characterized the Brighton Odeon (*above right*), which Andrew Mather created for Oscar Deutsch's chain in 1937. Stepped towers flanked the entrance of Gaston Leroux's *c.*1932-35 Théâtre de Villeurbanne, Lyons (*opposite below*), a far cry from high-style Paris Moderne of a decade earlier, while a single right-hand tower distinguished the Palmarium in Tunis (*below right*), whose name was spelled out with bold Moderne lettering.

One of the grandest Art Deco waterfront structures was Nice's so-called 'Palais de la Mediterranée' (*opposite*). The 1927-28 marble and stucco casino-playground was designed by Charles Dalmas and is still a strong presence on the Promenade des Anglais.

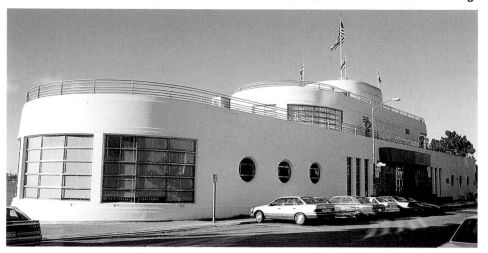

Built in 1939 as Hoffman's Cafeteria (and later a ballroom and disco), the China Club (*right centre*) is one of Miami Beach's most dramatic Streamline Moderne structures; its architect was Henry Hohauser. An appropriately nautical/ Streamline Moderne appearance was given to San Francisco's National Maritime Museum (*right above*) designed by William Mooser Sen. and William Mooser Jr. in 1939. Streamlined curves also informed the nineteen-thirties seaside pavilion at Ocean Beach in New London, Connecticut (*right below*); decorative roundels on its façade portrayed a whale, sea horse and fish.

Yet more Moderne entertainment palaces, on three continents: Henry White's 1927 Palais Pictures (*left*), later the Palais Theatre, part of the amusement halls at St. Kilda Beach, Melbourne; the auditorium at Vierzon, France (*below left*); the Kino Gdynia in Lódź, Poland (*below*); the Casino in Madras, India (*opposite above*); and the spectacular, fountain-like Gaumont Palace in Paris (*opposite below left*) by Henri Belloc, which, along with John Eberson and Auguste Bluysen's Rex, was one of the French capital's two premier Moderne cinemas; dating from 1931, the Rex was demolished in 1972.

Like world fairs, amusement parks in the twenties and thirties often included fantasy architecture that took *le style moderne* to dizzying, decorative heights. Unlike temporary exhibition pavilions, however, arcades, rides, stalls and other architectural fun-fair attractions, such as the 'Auto Skooter' bumper cars at Denver's Lakeside Park (*above*), housed in a smart Streamline Moderne enclosure, generally had longer lives.

165

One of the most lavish seaside entertainment centres was the Palais de la Mediterranée (Charles Dalmas, 1927-28), the two-acre playground American multi-millionaire Frank Jay Gould built along Nice's Promenade des Anglais. Its massive marble and stucco façade was that of a white-washed Moderne temple, with side sections displaying stylized Neoclassical tableaux. Joseph Emberton's Blackpool Casino (1938-39) was a markedly different gamblers' haunt, with a lively vertical sign abutting a tall, spiralling staircase.

Smaller poolside structures, too, came in Art Deco packages, such as those at the Kearney Pool in Kearney, Nebraska (1936); the Green Hill Farms Hotel in Philadelphia (c.1929); and the Arizona Biltmore, Phoenix. Regent's Park Zoo in London contains perhaps Britain's best-known and -loved Streamline Moderne 'structure': the Penguin Pool (Berthold Lubetkin and Tecton, 1933–34) – all white, sculptural, stepped, spiralling and cantilevered.

Private clubs and associations across the United States opted for Moderne rather than traditional looks for their clubhouses or headquarters, though some, like the massive Elks Temple in Los Angeles (Curlett & Beelman, 1925), included traditional symbolic elements around the façade. A small gem of an Art Deco building, arguably Connecticut's finest, is the Polish National Home in Hartford (Henry F. Ludorf, 1930), which features a wealth of carved and forged ornament on its buff brick-covered four sides. Form alone, rather than applied decoration, distinguished the handsome Women's City Club in St. Paul, Minnesota (Magnus Jemme, c.1932); large fluted cylindrical segments and stepped sections, along with wraparound windows, gave it an elegant Moderne silhouette.

Travel Buildings

Streamlined, aerodynamic, thoroughly modern images were strongly expressive of increased opportunities in travel in the twenties and thirties. From sleek locomotives and gleaming automobile bodies to giant-prowed ocean liners and bullet-like dirigibles, methods of modern travel conjured up a new vocabulary of images. Consequently, transportation-connected buildings were prime subjects to which architects could give Moderne forms or elements of the streamline type.

Colourful, decorated structures like Otto Wagner's Karlsplatz station in Vienna (1898–99) and Eliel Saarinen's Helskinki Railroad Station (1904–14) paved the way for exuberant Art Deco-period railroad termini. One of the grandest was Milan's Stazione Centrale (Eugenio Montuori, 1931), a massive stone pile that followed in the tradition of monumental Italian architecture, but also possessed Moderne elements, including geometric motifs and stylized animal and human figures.

In the United States, the Cincinnati Union Terminal (Roland Anthony Wank & Paul Philippe Cret, for Fellheimer & Wagner, 1929–33) was a huge domed concrete pile. The gently stepped exterior, though not as ornate as the interior, contained two massive figural reliefs and, supporting the huge numberless clock, a pair of stepped pilasters. The same firm also designed the New York Central Terminal in Buffalo (1927–29), which comprised a domed as well as stepped multi-storey structure. The stepped, Cubist mass making up the glazed-terracotta Omaha Union Station in Nebraska (Gilbert S. Underwood, 1929–30) included Moderne relief decoration, such as the figure-surmounted pilasters flanking the entrances, reminiscent of the sculptures on Helsinki Railroad Station. The massive Texas & Pacific Passenger Terminal and Warehouse Buildings complex in Fort Worth (Wyatt C. Hedrick, with Herman C. Koeppe, 1931) was an encyclopedia of Art Deco ornament, with added neo-Gothic, Native American, classical and Egyptian elements. Huge surface areas of the thirteen-storey passenger terminal and eight-storey warehouse – door and window surrounds, spandrels, turrets and cornices – were covered with volutes, urns, blossoms, zigzags, stepped diamonds, stylized eagles or patterned brickwork. A world apart from this ornate mass was the modest, framed-stucco Southern Pacific Train Station in Casa Grande, Arizona (William F. Meaney, 1939–40), a Pueblo Deco structure set with running arrows (sideways chevrons) and truncated pyramids (Navajo cloud symbols) in polychrome cast concrete. Las Vegas's Union Pacific Depot was in the Streamline Moderne vein; its boxy form was enlivened with a curved fin at the top, on which a sign was perched, and a semicircular wing was bordered all round with a supported awning.

In Britain, London Underground stations were designed in a modified Moderne manner in the twenties and thirties, most under the direction of Charles Holden (1875–1960), of Adams, Holden & Pearson (which designed the London Passenger Transport Board's headquarters in 1926–29). Just as Oscar Deutsch wished to present the public with a chain of 'user-friendly', easily identifiable cinemas, so Frank Pick, director of the London Passenger Transport Board, wanted a well-designed, appealing Tube station. The first design was the two-storey Clapham South (then Nightingale Lane) station of 1925–26, a limestone mass with a tri-faceted façade containing several examples of the Underground logo (a red ring bisected by a horizontal blue line): as two projecting signs, in coloured glass on a window and as capitals atop two pilasters. By 1930, Holden had full responsibility for designing more new stations, and the results – of which the red brick box topped with a cylindrical drum or tower is the most familiar – were Arnos Grove, the Moderne-turreted Boston Manor, Osterley and Park Royal.

Three 1932–33 City of New York substations (containing machines for converting direct current from alternating current for the Independent Subway) were attractive Art Deco structures. The Central Substation (West 53rd Street), Greenwich Substation (West 13th Street) and Smith Street Substation, Brooklyn, were brick boxes punctuated with Moderne grillework and light-hued frosting in the guise of door frames, pediments, bands, cornices and capitals adorned with zigzags, waves, chevrons, ziggurats and period letters.

From the nineteen-thirties the Greyhound Bus Depot was a fixture on the American landscape. Most stations were stepped or streamlined symmetrical buildings, crowned with a vertical streamlined sign atop which the company's famous logo, a speeding chrome greyhound, was situated. The reason for the uniformity of many depots was that they were designed by Wischmeyer, Arrasmith & Elswick, a Louisville, Kentucky, architectural firm. W.S. Arrasmith created over a hundred variations on the basic terminal, and these were built all over the country. Popular modern building materials, such as glass bricks, chromed-metal or aluminium banding, and terracotta and Vitrolite panels, were often used, and the house colours (as on the buses) were silver, blue and white. A handsome Arrasmith design was the *c.*1940 terminal in Washington, D.C., a four-stepped, white limestone structure with a pleasing blend of streamlined corners and black terracotta trim. The 1941 Baltimore depot included both curved and rectilinear corners; it was faced with buff concrete and highlighted with black stone and brick.

In Britain, two quite dissimilar coach stations were built in the Art Deco period. Green Line commissioned Gordon Jeeves to design its Poland Street station, which opened in 1930. A hastily designed and built rectangle with a stepped central segment, the station featured a jazzy zigzag and diamond cornice motif in vivid green tiles and Moderne neon lettering; it was in use for only three years, however, due to its congested location. By contrast, London's massive, streamlined Victoria Coach Station (Wallis, Gilbert & Partners, 1932) with its tall central tower straddling Buckingham Palace Road and Elizabeth Street, was a success.

The petrol or filling station was yet another Machine Age building phenomenon. In the nineteen-twenties and thirties there were Colonial Revival and Spanish Mission filling stations in the United States, but most common were Art Deco variants, with zigzag and streamlined elements predominating. As with Greyhound, there were 'house styles' for some petroleum companies. Texaco hired industrial designer Walter Dorwin Teague to create variations on the same Texaco station theme, and by 1940 over 500 versions of his 'standardized' 1936 designs were built, all featuring the familiar red lettering and Texaco red star. Gulf, too, had architects create for them a standard filling station, which included streamlined corners, horizontal steel bands, a large retail-display area with a curved-glass window and a stepped entrance tower set with glass bricks. All Gulf stations did not of course adhere to this pattern, an exotic exception being a cream-panelled, polychrome-enhanced example in Bedford, Pennsylvania, its form and decoration likening it to an Egyptian temple.

The independent filling station owner could choose from numerous forms and materials, with Vitrolite, glass bricks, coloured terracotta, aluminium and porcelain panels favoured. The latter prefabricated metal skins predominated as petrol-station sheathing in the thirties, not only in the United States but in Australia, where a 1939 advertisement recommended porcelain enamelled steel sheathing for filling stations, since it was 'corrosion-resisting and age-proof' and would 'not crack, craze or lose its

American petrol stations were ideal for bold Moderne decoration, such as a *c.*1934 Mobil service station in Los Angeles, topped by a tiered confection that resembled a stylized fountain.

This *c.*1930 American Gulf petrol station featured Moderne polychrome terracotta panels and a stepped central kiosk.

lustre'. There were interesting variations on the basic service station design throughout the United States. Miami Beach's Firestone Station (Zurwelle and Whitaker, 1939), with a massive cantilevered awning, took the resort town's overwindow eyebrow device to the limit. In Los Angeles, the circular-section retail area of a c.1934 Mobil Service Station was topped by a wedding-cake-like tower. A rectilinear, stepped Diamond Gas Station in Sapulpa, Oklahoma (Donald McCormick, c.1928–29), was an elegant black and cream Vitrolite exercise in its name: there were diamonds on the stepped black pumps and diamonds over the doors.

Other automobile-related buildings designed in the Art Deco mode included the Daimler Car Hire Garage (Wallis, Gilbert & Partners, 1931) London, a reinforced-concrete, mostly Modernist structure, but with some Moderne trim, and the Kent Columbus Circle Garage in Manhattan (Jardine, Hill & Murdock, 1929–30), a multi-storey 'automated parking garage', its gold-brick surface decorated with dark brick vertical strips, stepped triangles and horizontal bands, as well as blue and cream terracotta chevrons, diamonds and ziggurats. New York's Packard Motor Car Company Service Building (Albert Kahn with Frank S. Parker, c.1929) was a simple boxy form, but with ornate metal spandrels and polychrome terracotta masks and rosettes with a vaguely Greco-Mayan mien gave a bland warehouse-type building a distinctive look.

Most bridges, tunnels and roads qualify as civic structures, but they also relate to auto (and rail) travel. Herbert J. Rowse's Mersey Tunnel project was the finest complex of Art Deco civic-cum-travel structures in Britain: the tunnel entrances contained scalloped bands, stylized avian reliefs, zigzag borders and ornate metalwork. In the United States, the monumental pylons of the Soldiers and Sailors Memorial Bridge in Harrisburg, Pennsylvania (Gehron & Ross, c.1930–31), were topped by Lee Lawrie's stylized eagles and the limestone-faced, concrete-arched Calvert Street Bridge in Washington, D.C. (Paul Philippe Cret and Ralph Modjeski, 1935), today the Duke Ellington Bridge, bore the sculpted panels of classical deities by Leon Hermant, one a voluptuous half-naked goddess perched on the running board of a thirties automobile. In Connecticut, several bridges on the scenic-route Merritt and Wilbur Cross Parkways were Art Deco in style, at least one in the white-washed Streamline Moderne vein and others of simpler stepped-pier forms. Two world-renowned spans, the Sydney Harbour Bridge (1932) and the San Francisco-Oakland Bay Bridge (1939), include towering, stepped stone pylons of simple, monumental Art Deco form.

Some nineteen-twenties and thirties French and English ocean liners were floating Art Deco palaces, so it stands to reason that some nautical-related structures of the period took on aspects of the style. Piers 88, 90, and 92 on the Hudson River in New York, for instance, were built in 1935 and bore various Art Deco motifs. The Cunard Line's Pier 92 had dark stone ziggurats over its doors, and one large stepped segment rising over the roof line in the centre; zigzags, scrolls, sunburst and stepped diamonds also appeared.

Strong polychrome elements informed many travel-related Art Deco structures, whose forms ranged from the massive classical pile to the white-washed, streamlined confection. To the former category belongs the 1930 Suburban Station of the Pennsylvania Railroad in Philadelphia (*above*), its elegant façade like a huge oynx, ruby and gold brooch; its architects, Graham, Anderson, Probst & White, also designed the city's grand stripped-Neoclassical 30th Street Station. A dramatic cantilevered awning – an exaggerated 'eyebrow' – caps the entry porch of the Firestone service station in Miami Beach (*opposite below*), designed in 1939 by engineers Zurwelle and Whitaker. In the July 1930 issue of *Architecture*, the Hanley Company of Bradford, Pennsylvania, advertised its polychrome slip-glazed brick as ideal cladding for modern filling stations (*opposite above*): Vahan Hagopian was the artist of this handsome rendering.

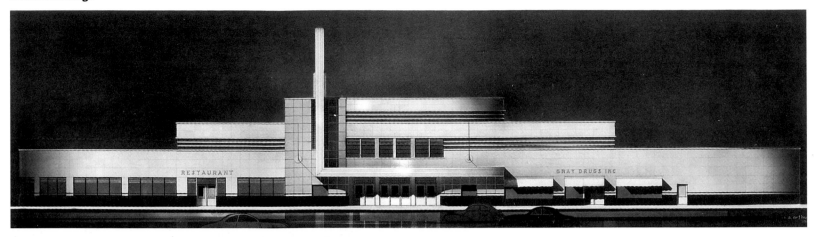

GREYHOUND TERMINAL WASHINGTON D. C.
WISCHMEYER ARRASMITH & ELSWICK ARCHITECTS

The Louisville, Kentucky, architectural firm founded in 1926 as Wischmeyer & Arrasmith created hundreds of Greyhound Bus Terminals from 1937 to 1972. Many of W.S. Arrasmith's finest thirties designs were of the low, single-towered variety, as seen in his sleek plans (drawn by S. Arthur) for Streamline Moderne depots in Cleveland (*above*), dated 1946, and Washington, D.C. (*left*), 1938.

Charles Holden's varied but distinctive designs for London Underground stations created severe, angular piles, such as the 1932 Morden station (*centre*), long, single-turreted, brick boxes, such as the 1934 Boston Manor station (*above*), and the cylinder-topped variety, as at Arnos Grove (*below*), 1932. Despite their disparate faces, all were easily identified by a large, prominently placed Underground logo (a red ring bisected by a blue line).

Considered a last gasp of London Moderne, the Imperial Airways building (*below left*), later headquarters of B.O.A.C. and British Airways (and now of the National Audit Office), went up in 1939; its architect was Albert Lakeman, and the monumental winged figures were by E.R. Broadbent. Much smaller but still striking was the 1930 Green Line coach station (*below right*) in Poland Street, London, by Gordon Jeeves, co-designer of Ideal House (see page 14). He added similar pseudo-Moorish touches to this edifice, including an exotic 'valance' executed in green tiles; the depot was open for only three years.

The old East Side Airlines Building in Manhattan (*above*) was a latter-day temple of commerce and transportation, a massive stone box surmounted by a pair of Moderne eagles. The 1939-40 building is no longer extant, but before demolition the birds were rescued; they now stand guard at the entrance of the modern glass box that is the corporate headquarters of Best Products in Richmond, Virginia (*left*).

The heyday of rail travel is long gone in the United States, but thankfully some superb Art Deco train stations still remain. Once scheduled for demolition, the 1929-33 Cincinnati Union Terminal (*opposite below*) has been revived as a cultural and entertainment complex (incorporating a working train station); its designers were Roland Anthony Wank and Paul Philippe Cret, for Fellheimer & Wagner. The 1931 Tulsa Union Depot (*opposite above*), created by R.C. Stevens, today functions as the offices of the WilTel telecommunications group.

In Basra, Iraq, a 1929 design for a raised-domed, twin-towered Port Office (J.M. Wilson) combined traditional Mesopotamian motifs with Moderne ones. In Oran, Algeria, however, the structures built along the *paquebot* berths were strictly rectilinear-Moderne, including a soaring clock tower that Mallet-Stevens would have admired. Albert Kahn designed the William Livingstone Memorial Lighthouse on Belle Isle, Michigan (*c.*1930). A sleek, square-section, fluted marble column set on a stepped base and adorned with figural sculptures by Geza Maroti, the lighthouse was a far cry from the generic American building type. Four pairs of two columns surmounted the stepped limestone mass, these in turn topped by a conical, octagonal roof. Although the memorial plaque to Livingstone was traditionally rendered, the overall image of the lighthouse given to mariners would be startlingly Moderne.

Structures directly related to air travel, such as hangars, airports and aerodromes, did not generally lend themselves to highly decorated flights of fancy, but there were Streamline Moderne edifices of this type. In Britain, such airports included those at Ramsgate (David Pleydell-Bouverie, 1936–37), whose long, narrow, curved-sided form likened it to an aeroplane's wing span; Croydon, whose ancillary aircraft factory had a stepped clock tower; and Shoreham (Stavers H. Tiltman, 1936). The stepped-cylinder control tower of the Birmingham Aerodrome (Norman & Dawbarn, 1938–39) sported massive projecting side canopies that resembled wings. Though generally considered International Style, the comma-shaped Dublin Airport (Desmond FitzGerald and the Office of Public Works, 1936–40) possesses white-washed projecting and cantilevered elements found in Streamline Moderne buildings.

L.V. Lacy's hangar design at the Wyoming Valley Airport in Wilkes-Barre, Pennsylvania (*c.*1929), featured a Moderne tower, while Kenneth Franzheim's Roosevelt Field, on Long Island, New York (*c.*1929), was decorated with zigzags, scrolls, stepped segments and a stylized eagle. Fort Worth's Municipal Airport Administration Building (Wiley G. Clarkson, 1937) was a long, two-storey, reinforced-concrete structure, its highlight a two-stepped, faceted glass and aluminium control tower emerging from a central cylindrical section with a zigzag band. Much smaller was Montana's Great Falls Airport (*c.*1939), made up of cylindrical sections, curved sides and a squared-off turret over a soaring entrance.

Civic Structures

A wide range of Art Deco municipal and federal structures were built, among them town halls, state and national capitols, fire stations, courthouses, embassies, monuments, dams, tunnels and any number of government-funded projects.

Regarding town halls and other municipal designs of the popular clock tower type, there were two significant models that seemed to be most influential on later architects. One was Willem Marinus Dudok's Hilversum Town Hall (1924–30), the finest example of the Dutch architect's distinctive

civic style, which in turn had been informed by the designs of Frank Lloyd Wright. The golden brick-sheathed Town Hall, like many Dudok projects, comprised a largely symmetrical massing of small and large brick cubes and rectangles that resulted in a lightness, even warmth, vis-à-vis their juxtaposition of horizontals and verticals. The building's design also made some reference to the Amsterdam School and De Stijl, as well as to Ragnar Östberg's 1920–23 City Hall in Stockholm, which influenced others, such as Arne Jacobsen and Erik Møller and their Århus, Denmark, Town Hall (1937–42). Scandinavians were fond of this building type, as evidenced by Arnstein Arneberg and Magnus Poulsson's Oslo City Hall (1917–50), a lavish Beaux-Arts-cum-Moderne brick pile. Germans, too, updated this basic municipal structure, as in Fritz Höger's Town Hall at Rustringen (1929–30), Expressionist but with some elements relating to Art Deco. In Great Britain, several buildings echoed Dudok's earlier design, including the rectilinear brick town hall at Hornsey (Reginald Uren, Slater & Moberley, 1935–37) and that in Greenwich (Clifford Culpin, 1939).

The other highly influential municipal structure was Bertram Grosvenor Goodhue's Nebraska State Capitol, Lincoln (*c.*1920–32). This setback, golden-domed tower sat on a broad, square base and featured a huge arched entryway; its clean-lined massive segments were nicely integrated, as were its classical and Moderne forms and ornament. Its façade was decorated by Lee Lawrie and others with apposite historical, regional and symbolic motifs and themes in high- and low-relief carving. American buildings influenced by Goodhue's tower included Los Angeles City Hall (John C. Austin, John Parkinson & Albert C. Martin, 1926–28), a Mayan pyramidal-roofed, 28-storey-high skyscraper towering over a rectangular mass, and the Louisiana State Capitol in Baton Rouge (1933), designed by the New Orleans firm of Weiss, Dreyfous & Seiferth, with considerable input from Governor Huey Long. An extensive sculptural programme on its façade depicted Louisiana state history and Mardi Gras celebrations alike, as well as geometric motifs and indigenous flora and fauna; especially handsome were Ulric Ellerhusen's huge allegorical figures near the tower's top. Another notable state capitol was Francis Keally's in Salem, Oregon (1936–38), its long, flat mass topped by a cylindrical drum-like tower.

Many American courthouses, even some jails, were designed in the classical-Moderne mode, including the Ector County Courthouse in Texas (E. Withers, 1938), a single-stepped box decorated near the top with reliefs of two bold stylized equestrian figures; the Racine County Courthouse in Wisconsin (Holabird & Root, *c.*1931), a restrained, multi-setback box with sculptural accents at its upper sections; the ziggurat-towered Bronx County Jail (Max Hausle & Joseph H. Freedlander, *c.*1931); Manhattan's House of Detention for Women (Sloan & Robertson, 1929–30) with lively textured brickwork done in the Amsterdam School manner; and the Camden County Courthouse and City Hall in New Jersey (Edwards & Green, *c.*1931), much in the Nebraska State Capitol mould, with stunning Native American eagle, chevron and other Moderne motifs on its metal doors and elsewhere.

An important model for American civic structures was Bertram Grosvenor Goodhue's Nebraska State Capitol (see page 181). Along the same lines as that broad-based, central-towered stone mass was the 1926-28 Los Angeles City Hall (*below*) by John C. Austin, John Parkinson and Albert C. Martin; unlike the gold-domed Goodhue project, it featured a Mayan pyramid roof. In New Jersey, the *c.*1931 Camden County Courthouse and City Hall (*opposite*) by Edwards & Green, featured handsome Moderne metalwork (including doors with Native American and geometric motifs). On the other side of the Atlantic, Charles Holden designed the 1932-37 Senate House of the University of London (*right*) as a finely proportioned, Portland stone-clad stepped mass.

Civic Structures

Bertram Grosvenor Goodhue's influential Nebraska State Capitol at Lincoln (*opposite*), dating from *c.*1920-32, set an example for numerous civic structures throughout the country, including the 1933 Louisiana Capitol in Baton Rouge (*right*), designed by Weiss, Dreyfous & Seiferth of New Orleans. The two shared similar monumental forms, as well as the talents of sculptor Lee Lawrie. The elaborate sculptural programmes on and around these and other such buildings often had direct relevance to the region or state, such as 'The Sower' topping Goodhue's golden dome (the building's setting was fertile Nebraska farm country) and, echoing the Louisiana tower's form, the 1940 memorial to Governor Huey Long, who had initiated the Capitol project.

Both original subjects and stock Art Deco motifs enhanced many educational institutions in the United States. In New York City, Hermann Ridder Junior High School, otherwise known as Public School (P.S.) 98 (*left*), featured figure-topped pilasters over the entrance tower and, along its two sides, a row of stepped parapets.

Civil architect Willem Marinus Dudok's 1924-30 Town Hall in Hilversum, the Netherlands (*above*), was an important influence for many civic structures in Europe. Influenced by the works of Frank Lloyd Wright, among others, Dudok created this golden-brick complex as a pleasing, cohesive mass of horizontal and vertical elements.

The Tulsa State Fairgrounds (*right top*) were enhanced with exuberant polychrome ornament, in this case horse heads amid stylized flora. A variety of stock Deco motifs, including zigzags, scrolls, and alate and floral forms, decorated the 1936 Will Rogers Memorial Coliseum, Tower and Auditorium in Fort Worth, Texas (*right centre above*), part of the Frontier Centennial Exposition, designed by Wyatt C. Hedrick and Elmer G. Withers. P.W.A. or Classic

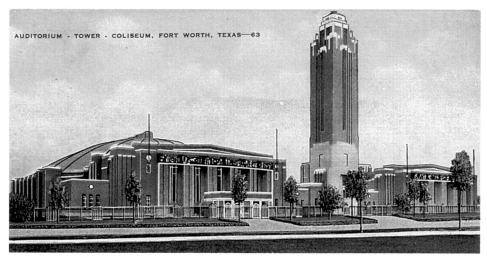

AUDITORIUM - TOWER - COLISEUM, FORT WORTH, TEXAS—63

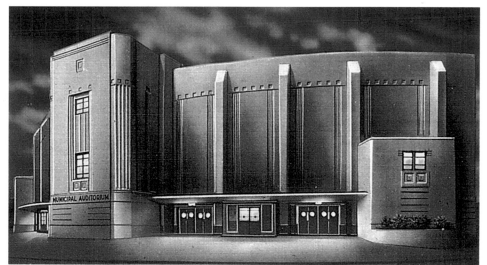

MUNICIPAL AUDITORIUM

Moderne was the appellation often applied to massive public projects such as the Municipal Auditorium at Charleston, West Virginia (*right centre below*), and that at Sioux City, Iowa (*right below*). Both included classical architectural elements, but treated in a modern, shorthand manner, for instance, substituting simple piers for columns with elaborate bases and capitals.

Herbert J. Rowse's towering ventilation station (one of six) of the 1934 Mersey Tunnel in Liverpool (*above*) stands out as a bold, decorated civic skyscraper. In Los Angeles, Morgan, Walls & Clements designed the Thomas Jefferson High School (*above left*) in 1936, while Berthold Lubetkin and Tecton created the sleek, abundantly glazed Finsbury Health Centre in London (*below left*), admittedly more Modernist than Moderne, in 1938. Lubetkin designed one

of the British capital's best-loved 'waterfront complexes': the 1934 Penguin Pool (*above right*) at London Zoo in Regent's Park, a part-Moderne, part-International Style structure. In Paris's 13th *arrondissement*, an unusual stepped, cylindrical school in the Rue Kuss (*below right*) was designed by Roger-Henri Expert in 1934. Expert contributed to the design of the *Normandie* ocean liner, so the institution's decidedly nautical bent is not surprising.

186

The exuberantly decorated Polish National Home in Hartford, Connecticut (*opposite above right*), one of the finest (and best preserved) Art Deco buildings in the state, was designed by Henry F. Ludorf in 1930. Its buff brick-clad form included a wealth of carved and forged Moderne ornament, including some in polychromy.

The forms of the Joan of Arc Junior High School in New York (*opposite left*) and St Mary's grammar school in Middletown, Connecticut (*opposite centre right*), are fairly undistinguished as buildings, but the decorative elements at their entrances are boldly Moderne. The narrow, elongated sculptural panel on the Manhattan public school (Eric Kebbon, 1939-40) depicts a snaking plant surrounded by grapes and blossoms, while the lower brownstone façade of the 1930 grammar school features Moderne lettering, a zigzag band and an unusual spider-web motif (which did appear on other Art Deco buildings, but only rarely).

In addition to their light-stone façades, Pueblo Deco structures in the American Southwest made use of various decorative devices derived from both the Native American and standard Moderne repertoires. The Federal Building in Albuquerque (*opposite below right*) combined Hopi and Navajo motifs with Hispanic ones; this overdoor detail shows a stylized thunderbird and other avian designs. Also in the New Mexico city, the pastel-sheathed Indian Hospital (originally a tuberculosis sanitorium) of 1934 (*right*) is a setback, pyramidal structure, including Native American cloud and geometric patterns; its architect was Hans Stamm.

Major civil engineering projects, including bridges, tunnels and dams, were built on Moderne lines on both sides of the Atlantic. About 1927 architect Charles L. Morgan suggested a 'rainbow skyscraper bridge' (*opposite left*) for Chicago. Herbert J. Rowse's 1934 Mersey Tunnel included ventilation towers and entrances (*opposite above right*) with smart Moderne motifs, while a much simpler arch supported the upper level of the Western Hills viaduct at Spring Grove Avenue in Cincinnati, Ohio (*opposite below right*).

One of the most ambitious American civil engineering projects of the thirties, the Hoover Dam (*right*), at Lake Mead, was supervised by chief engineer A.H. Ayers. The Moderne elements of the massive complex were mainly due to Gordon B. Kaufmann, the Los Angeles architect engaged by the U.S. Bureau of Reclamation to update the classical ornament first planned for the Arizona-Nevada dam. Kaufmann also oversaw the competition for the dam memorial, which resulted in Oskar J.W. Hansen's 1935-38 bronze figures (*above*), known as 'The Spirit of Man' or 'Winged Figures of the Republic'.

The Pueblo Deco style was used for several significant courthouses. The Potter County Courthouse in Amarillo, Texas (Townes, Lightfoot & Funk, 1932), was quite similar in shape to the aforementioned Racine building, but its relief sculptures, such as a frontiersman, ox yoke and prickly pear cacti, were of regional interest. The U.S. Courthouse in Fort Worth was designed by Paul Philippe Cret in 1933; it, too, contained Native American motifs, no more profusely than on the aluminium grilles, spandrels and other metalwork, which included stepped pyramids, zigzags and scalloped lines. The Cochise County Courthouse in Bisbee, Arizona (Roy Place, 1931), featured cast-concrete stylized cactus spandrels and two bronze figures of Justice in a sunray surround on the doors.

In Europe, the white granite-faced Government Buildings in Dublin (J.R. Boyd Barrett, 1935–38) comprised a basic stripped-Neoclassical mass, but with an Art Deco entrance bay including a bas-relief over the door, zigzag spandrels and a Moderne mask of a woman's face. The Federal Building in Balboa Park, San Diego (Richard Requa), could not present a more anti-thetical face: built for the 1935 California-Pacific International Exposition, its direct inspiration was the Governor's Palace at Uxmal. A dense ornamental band, with a mask at its centre, was over the door. The Albuquerque Federal Building's inspiration was more general: its façade featured much Native American ornament, especially the thunderbird.

Several foreign embassies and other such buildings, especially French or French colonial, were built in the Art Deco style. The French Legation in Belgrade (Roger-Henri Expert, 1934) was a monumental-Moderne structure featuring Carlos Sarrabezolles sculptures. In Algeria, the Maison du Colon in Mascara (1938) was a modified stepped structure with reliefs, metalwork and lettering in the Moderne style, and Oran's Maison de l'Agriculture boasted a three-sided corner façade covered with bas-reliefs.

Schools, libraries, museums and other buildings related to learning and culture were designed with various Moderne aspects, notably bas-reliefs and carvings. Most such institutions were of traditional, function-first forms, but they might feature an ornamental band of scrolls or zigzags, stylized-floral panel, sunburst window or, most commonly, Moderne lettering, as on the 1930 grammar school, St Mary of Czestochowa, in Middletown, Connecticut, whose unremarkable form was given a quasi-jazzy façade with Deco lettering, an overdoor zigzag band and a spider-web design.

W.P.A labourers helped build large numbers of Moderne schools throughout the United States, including the sprawling, stepped North Side Senior High School in Fort Worth (Wiley G. Clarkson, 1937). Stylized scrolls, fluting, fountain motifs, wavy and scalloped bands, and diamonds featured among the cast-stone designs on the cream-brick façade. A horizontal mass with two side wings, Baltimore's Garrison Junior High School (Smith & May, 1931) was capped with geometric and floral cast-concrete trim; a wealth of detail on the central tower resembled so much white icing on red brick. Two notable Washington, D.C., area schools were George Washington High School in Alexandria, Virginia (Raymond Long, 1935), its entry comprising

During Prohibition, the old Peter Ballantine Brewery in Newark became the New Jersey Law School, its remodelled entrance covered with stylized Moderne motifs, as well as bas-relief figures and objects symbolic of Truth, Justice and Knowledge.

Paul Philippe Cret's Folger Shakespeare Library in Washington, D.C., was a sober stone pile of 1932, designed in collaboration with Alexander B. Trowbridge. Often referred to as 'Greco Deco', the clean-lined, classically proportioned pile nonetheless included strong modern statements in its abundant use of cast aluminium (for windows, grilles and railings) and its novel ground-level placement of nine bas-relief panels depicting scenes from Shakespearian plays.

three fluted piers that terminated above the roof as rounded fins in a stepped motif, and the Streamline Moderne Greenbelt Center Elementary School in Maryland (Douglas Ellington & Reginald D. Wadsworth, 1936), set with bas-relief panels illustrating the clauses of the Preamble to the Constitution. Appropriate decoration featured on the cornice of the Biology Institute building at Harvard University (Coolidge, Shepley, Bullfinch & Abbott, c.1932): a hand-carved brick frieze of elephants. A lofty allegorical group made up of Truth and Justice featured over the entrance of the New Jersey Law School in Newark, which in the early thirties was remodelled out of the old Peter Ballantine Brewery. Black, green, tan, blue, sienna and orange terracotta was used in the vignette, which depicted four figures in a high-style Parisian setting that included a fountain, floral urn, wavy clouds and sunburst. Colour, including blue terracotta panels, was a prime component of the jazzy façade of Bloom High School in Chicago Heights, Illinois (Royer, Danelli & Smith, 1931), a veritable encyclopedia of Art Deco: zigzag, chevron and wave patterns, stepped segments, foliate spandrels and figural sculpture (seated students of stone).

Thomas Jefferson High School in Los Angeles (Morgan, Walls & Clements, 1936) was pure Streamline Moderne. A wide array of Neoclassical-Moderne relief sculpture appeared on South Pasadena High School (Norman Marsh, David Smith & Herbert Powell, 1935–36; Merrell Gage, sculptor); Lou Henry Hoover School, Whittier (William Henry Harrison, 1938; Bartolo Mako, sculptor); and Hollywood High School (Marsh, Smith & Powell, 1934–35; Merrell Gage and Bartolo Mako, sculptors).

In Britain, the finely proportioned, stepped mass of Charles Holden's Senate House of the University of London (1932–37) is remarkable for its attention to detail, rich Portland-stone façade and pair of gargoyle-like sculptures, on the north and south elevations. More in the Dudok idiom were Bedford Girls' Modern School (Oswald P. Milne) and H.W. Burchett's Greenford County Secondary Grammar School in Middlesex, both handsome thirties brick blends of rectilinear and rounded elements with towers.

A notable Streamline Moderne school in France was Roger-Henri Expert's Ecole Communale in the Rue Kuss, Paris (1934). Its dramatic form comprised four setback, stepped cylinders circled with metal railings and centring square sections; at the top was a rectilinear tower. Expert's nautical work (he helped fit out the *Normandie*) was evoked with this form. Another Paris school, in the Boulevard Berthier (A. Dresse & L. Oudin, with René Lecard, 1938), was akin to an Odeon, with two low side arms around a central section that featured a bas-relief of the arms of the City of Paris.

Of all the American libraries built in the thirties, two of the best known were in Washington, D.C.: the classically influenced Folger Shakespeare Library (Paul Philippe Cret, with Alexander Trowbridge, 1932) and the huge Library of Congress Annex (Pierson & Wilson, with Alexander Trowbridge, 1939). Often referred to as 'Greco Deco', the Folger was indeed a classically proportioned, clean-lined work, but it also acknowledged the present, with its nine classical-Moderne bas-relief panels and cast-aluminium grillework, balustrades and windows. The Library of Congress Annex has also been called Greco Deco; its finest Deco components are inside the grand, white-washed structure, but such external details as a stylized marble owl, Moderne lighting fixtures and abundant zigzag and fluted elements are noteworthy.

Also built in the Art Deco period was the Los Angeles Public Library (1922–26), a structure of roughly the same pyramidal-tower form as the nearby Los Angeles City Hall. This was not surprising, since City Hall's inspiration was in part taken from Bertram Goodhue's Nebraska State Capitol – and the architect of the library was Goodhue (with Curleton M. Winslow). The raised pyramid surmounting the library's tower is covered with glittering tiles, a shining rayed sun enclosed in a blue circle its salient feature. Various historical and mythological characters adorn the exterior, which is more exotic hybrid than Moderne. But American libraries were not all monumental piles: for instance, a boxy public library in Pine Bluffs, Arkansas (c.1935), was exuberant and inviting, a stylized sunburst window over the door, ziggurat motifs over windows, decorative spandrels and zigzag cornices. The Bass Museum of Art in Miami Beach, designed by Russell T. Pancoast, opened in 1930 as the Miami Beach Library and Art Center. The tripartite entrance of the stepped keystone building featured two Moderne wrought-iron sconces and three bas-relief panels by Gustav Bohland, the centre one a stylized pelican with palm fronds. Above the entrance were two sculptural groups of three seagulls perched one on top of another.

In Europe, an interesting modernization of a traditional form occurred in the four identical public libraries (1934–35) designed by the Dublin Corporation for the suburbs of Drumcondra, Inchicore, Phibsboro and Ringsend. The high-pitched roofs were traditional, but the libraries' entryways – stepped back, with ornamental metalwork and a zigzag border – were distinctly Moderne. Even the traditional Gaelic script was given a quasi-contemporary look.

The Royal Masonic Hospital in Ravenscourt Park, London (Sir John Burnet, Tait & Lorne, 1929–33), made a bold two-sided Moderne statement. Not only did the brick structure include innovative welded-steel, curved porches ('sun balconies') of nautical inspiration, but it also looked back to Dudok's Hilversum Hall by virtue of the Administration block's dramatic stepped entry, which included textured brickwork and a pair of elongated figural sculptures terminating above-door pilasters. The Hospital for Infectious Diseases, Paisley, another thirties project by Sir John Burnet, Tait & Lorne, comprised some dozen white-washed buildings in a verdant setting, many with streamlined corners, nautical railings and thick piers adorned with horizontal bands. On the other hand, a novel Modernist agenda was followed by Berthold Lubetkin and Tecton in the Finsbury Health Centre, London (1935–38), with its myriad glass bricks and facing tiles making it an exceptionally adventurous design for thirties London.

The Native American totem pole form was updated in quasi-Moderne manner (by Toronto architect John M. Lyle) and used as a door surround on the Runnymede Branch of the Toronto Public Library.

The dramatic entrance to the Royal Masonic Hospital in Ravenscourt Park, London (Sir John Burnet, Tait & Lorne, 1929-33) paid homage to Willem Marinus Dudok's Hilversum Town Hall; the London hospital had an added sculptural element in the two huge figures above the door.

In the United States, two significant military hospitals with a strong Art Deco bent were built in the nineteen-thirties. The U.S. Naval Hospital in Philadelphia (Walter T. Karcher & Livingston Smith, 1933–35) comprised a thirteen-storey, U-shaped structure sheathed in cream and buff brick, limestone and tiles. There was little external ornament, the aluminium trim, varicoloured brick and other surfaces providing a counterpoint to the form's rising pilasters, recessed windows and handsome free-standing piers surmounted by Moderne lamps. On the West Coast, the twelve-storey, centre-turreted U.S. Marine Hospital in Seattle (Bebb & Gould and John Graham, c.1935) also used varicoloured brick (in orange-brown and black shades) to provide decorative effects, but terracotta details, too, were added, such as copings, sills and decorative panels on the upper storeys (common motifs were zigzags and chevrons). Another related structure was the U.S. Navy Medical Center in Bethesda, Maryland (F.W. Southworth, with Paul Philippe Cret, 1940), its 22-storey-high, stepped tower making it the Washington area's first skyscraper. The Albuquerque Indian Hospital (Hans Stamm, 1934) was a cream-washed, multi-terraced and -stepped structure of a basic T form. Subtle Navajo motifs distinguished the pyramidal exterior, including fluted terracotta copings in turquoise (which denoted divine fertility in Pueblo colour symbolism).

Two somewhat similar (to each other) long, flat-roofed, white-washed structures were the City-County Hospital, Fort Worth (Wiley G. Clarkson, 1939), symmetrical yet not severe, with streamlined, rectilinear and Moderne-sculptural elements, and the thirties Miami Beach Hospital-Clinic, whose decoration comprised a dramatic parapet design of draped pilasters and spandrels and figural bas-reliefs.

Whether studded with stylized eagles, set with fancy metalwork or adorned with geometric or floral motifs from the classic Art Deco repertoire, branches of the U.S. Post Office built in the twenties and thirties were prime candidates for the Moderne treatment. They could be temple-like monumental structures or modest squares or cylinders. A good example of the latter was Miami Beach's Main Post Office (Howard L. Chesney, 1937), a stripped-down cylinder in the centre of square sections and topped with a lantern-tower. A classic monumental structure, with only a few Moderne touches (like the ubiquitous stylized eagle), was the huge Boston Post Office. Another eagle of a somewhat vestigial nature was carved *in situ* on the corner of the Main Post Office in Kansas City (James A. Wetmore, 1933–35). A courthouse was combined with a post office in a monumental pink marble pile in Knoxville, Tennessee (Baumann & Baumann, c.1935). Rainbow granite sheathed the balustrades and base and comprised the steps, and it also made up the entryway, which featured a double-scalloped border at top, aluminium grilles over the doors and, in the windows above, casements with a horizontal wave pattern and vertical lotus one.

Abroad, in Boghari, Algeria, a white-washed post and telegraph office (c.1930) included a tower and Moderne railing, and in Paris an accordion-pleat façade sheathed the front of the post office in the Champs-Elysées (Jean Desbouis, with Ledieu et Zipper, 1929). The motif was meant to be a beacon representing the radio station also within the building.

From California to New York, Moderne fire stations were built in the twenties and thirties. Engine Co. 1 in East Los Angeles (1940) was a simple white box enlivened by horizontal recesses, Moderne lettering and an L-shaped motif connecting the upper level of windows to the perpendicular door. There was also an impressive 1936 Art Deco fire station in Rochester, New York; carved on its main entrance portal were two twenty-foot-tall limestone firemen, and related equipment – hooks, ladders, fire hoses and chains – were sculpted on the façade. Handsome bas-reliefs (contemporary firefighters and fire-breathing dragons) also appeared on a terracotta frieze over the entrance to the Tulsa Fire Alarm Building. In Fort Worth, the Central Fire Station Headquarters and Fire Alarm Signal Station (Wyatt C. Hedrick, 1930) comprised, respectively, a huge square of a turreted building and a smaller adjacent box. Both were two storeys high, made of reinforced concrete and decorated with similar Moderne motifs, including patterned brickwork, terracotta scrolls and blossoms, and leaded-glass panels with a diamond and triangle design. In New Zealand, the old red brick Napier Fire Station (1921) featured complex stepped pyramid motifs dripping down and rising upwards from four large front piers. Horizontal fluting capped the smaller pilasters between the building's narrow windows.

Several major civil engineering-cum-building projects have been mentioned in previous sections, but one such type of structure has not yet been covered: the dam. Considered a prime example of American Art Deco architecture is the Hoover Dam near Boulder City, Nevada, built from 1930 to 1936 under the direction of chief engineer A.H. Ayers (of Arthur Powell Davis & Savage). The dam's massive curve of stone, punctuated with pylons and smaller ribs, was a dramatic, breathtaking sight, both an aesthetically pleasing architectural feat and a highly successful engineering endeavour. Its Streamline Moderne look was due to Gordon B. Kaufmann, whom the U.S. Bureau of Reclamation engaged to update the classical ornament originally planned for the dam. Kaufmann duly smoothed out the pylons, added setback towers at the highest point, redesigned the powerhouse and even created spillways in the streamlined vein. He also oversaw the competition for the dam memorial, which was won by Oskar J.W. Hansen, whose two thirty-feet-high winged bronze figures (1935–38) are as streamlined and unified as the engineering feat they honour.

Ecclesiastical architecture in Europe and North America included numerous examples in *le style moderne*. In the main traditional forms were tastefully adapted to modern tastes, with the usual Judaeo-Christian symbols, figures and themes duly conventionalized in the Art Deco manner.

In France, Moderne-era churches leaned towards Gothic and Romanesque shapes. Even the radically different churches designed by the Rationalist

Churches, Temples, Memorials and Monuments

architect, Auguste Perret (1874–1954), though innovative in terms of materials, were based on traditional forms. Notre Dame at Raincy, Paris (1922–23), his best-known church project, had Gothic roots, but its concrete cladding and glazing, with gridwork, circular and diamond patterns, was revolutionary ecclesiastical decoration.

Josef Goćár's Cathedral of Saint Wenceslaus in Prague was a dramatic form almost wholly modern in spirit: a huge bullnose apse, with a series of long vertical windows, led to a nave that stepped down dramatically in four setbacks, with the opposite end dominated by a stepped square tower. The Christian Science Church in The Hague (Hendrik P. Berlage, 1925), an obvious contemporary of Dudok's Hilversum Town Hall, was dominated by a squared-off clock tower that stood over an asymmetrical arrangement of brick buildings. Two notable Berlin churches were Ernst and Gunther Paulus's 1930 Kreuzkirche, a Gothic Expressionist three-stepped structure with tiers of relief zigzags under a rectangular tower, and Fritz Höger's Great Brick Church, Wilmersdorf, with an entry that stepped back and inwards and huge cylindrical piers.

One of the most influential buildings of the period was P.V. Jensen-Klint's Grundtvig Church, Copenhagen, begun in 1918 but not finished until 1940 (Klint's son, Kaare, took over after his father's death in 1930). The church's bold, heavenwards-bound silhouette updated the ziggurat-like shape of the Hanseatic stepped gable (also the usual form of southern Sweden's Skåne churches). Its roots were ages-old, yet the result was a bold Moderne-looking outline.

In the United Kingdom, both the Modern Movement and the Moderne manifested itself in churches, generally simple yet robust brick buildings, with perhaps one or two modern sculptural elements discreetly adorning the façade. Welch, Cachemaille-Day & Lander's St. Saviour, in Eltham, Kent (1932–33), was a much-praised square brick structure whose design paid homage to Albi cathedral in southern France. Its squat tower was not much higher than its flat roof, yet its dominant vertical elements, such as the long windows and triangular piers, created a strong upwards thrust. Another Welch, Cachemaille-Day & Lander design, St. Nicholas in Burnage, Manchester (1932), had a robust, neo-Romanesque form, but its curved and straight-angled elements were handled and decorated in a smart, contemporary way, the rounded apse featuring horizontal striping, the Cubist tower vertical bands. The Church of the Holy Cross in Greenford (A.E. Richardson, 1939) was constructed in a quasi-Streamline Moderne manner; one writer called it 'a modernistic Middlesex barn'. An unusual design by Sir E. Owen Williams was the Dollis Hill Synagogue (1937). One end of the main façade of the boxy building was simple and square, set with a multitude of shield-shaped windows, while the other was higher and comprised a three-dimensional zigzag, dominated by hexagonal windows enclosing a star of David.

In Cork, the Church of Christ the King (1927–31) by F. Barry Byrne (1904–82) was one of the finest ecclesiastical structures of the time in the

British Isles. The reinforced-concrete church was a transatlantic hybrid project, close in spirit to the Grundtvig Church in Denmark and created by an American who specialized in ecclesiastical buildings (and had worked with Frank Lloyd Wright). The plan of the Irish church was ambitious and innovative, with the entire octagonally shaped building stepped back from the façade. And the drama was increased by American sculptor John Storrs' Christ figure flanking the doors. Another Byrne design was Christ the King, Tulsa, Oklahoma, a 1925 Gothic-inspired church of rectangular form with hexagonal windows and a wealth of pinnacles.

There was another significant church in Tulsa, an oil-rich city that boasted a wealth of Art Deco architecture. The decoration of Boston Avenue Methodist Church (1928) had been attributed to its architect Bruce Goff, but it was largely created by Adah Robinson, Goff's teacher. The granite-based limestone structure featured a multitude of pinnacles and an abundance of symbolic stained glass and sculpture. Robinson's design programme reflected the desire of pastor John A. Rice to use a new set of symbols in his church; some Moderne motifs were praying hands, the seven-pointed star (for the seven virtues) and two indigenous flora, the torch lily (representing the church's strength and generosity) and the coreopsis (symbolic of the church's joy and hardiness).

Other Moderne religious structures in North America ranged from tiny meeting places (the Streamline Moderne Reading Room of the First Church of Christ Scientist in Winter Haven, Florida) to imposing modern temples (the Mormon Church in Cardston, Alberta, Canada, c.1931). Also in Canada, St. James Anglican Church in Vancouver (Adrian Gilbert Scott, 1935–37) was a Gothic Revival structure with stepped, angular and other Moderne references; surmounting its upper tower was a pyramidal roof that could have come from a Manhattan skyscraper. Martin Hedmark's First Swedish Baptist Church in New York (c.1931) was quite obviously indebted to the Grundtvig Church in Copenhagen, while the Church of Our Lady of Lourdes in Boyle Heights, Los Angeles (L.G. Scherer, 1930) was a mix of Spanish Mission and Art Deco. The First Baptist Church in Ventura, California (Robert B. Stacy-Judd, 1928–30), featured a soaring, ziggurat parapet, zigzag bands and stepped, triangular and fluted motifs. Two other Stacy-Judd projects, Los Angeles's Philosophical Research Center's auditorium (c.1935) and the Church of Jesus Christ of Latter-day Saints in Mexico City (1934), included Mexican palace-like towers and other Mayan motifs which regularly appeared in the architect's *oeuvre*.

In New York, the Church of the Heavenly Rest (Mayers, Murray & Philip, c.1929–30) in Fifth Avenue was Gothic Revival in form, with some exterior sculpture Moderne in spirit. The Fourth Church of Christ Scientist (Cherry & Matz, 1931–32), located in 181st Street in Manhattan, was a two-stepped square building decorated with zigzag bands and stylized foliate forms. The Church of the Most Precious Blood in Long Island City (Henry J. McGill, 1932) featured a superb Pueblo Deco interior; its exterior included stepped window frames and Moderne sculpture. McGill also designed the Shrine of

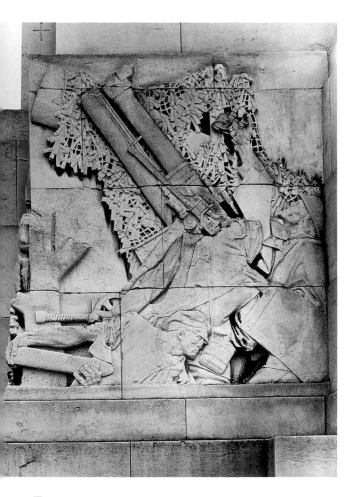

English sculptor Charles Sargeant Jagger's 1925 Royal Artillery Memorial In London's Hyde Park Corner includes bas-reliefs in a realistic yet unmistakably Moderne style.

the Little Flower in Royal Oak, Michigan (1933), whose Charity Crucifixion Tower was a densely carved free-standing tower with various figures and motifs surrounding a massive Christ on the cross; René Paul Chambellan was the sculptor.

Memorials, monuments, mausoleums and other sculptured 'structures' abounded in the interwar years, with the First World War bringing about hundreds of memorials, in Europe as well as North America and Australia. Probably the finest such Art Deco monument is the Anzac Memorial in Hyde Park, Sydney (C. Bruce Dellit, 1934). On each of the four sides of the imposing red granite memorial an amber window contains an image of the Anzac rising sun (which appears on the badge of the Australian military forces), and there is a stepped pyramid over the dome.

In the United States, several symbolic monuments of a Neoclassical bent contained Art Deco elements, such as the 1926 Liberty Memorial in Kansas City, Missouri, designed by Harold Van Buren Magonigle. Its focal element was a huge stone pillar, with monumental figures of Courage, Hope, Patriotism and Sacrifice carved towards the top; side structures included fountains and friezes, the latter with series of bas-reliefs and inscriptions honouring 'those who have dared bear the torches of sacrifice'. Paul Philippe Cret, the French-born Philadelphia architect, designed several war memorials in the United States and France. At Bellicourt, France, his early thirties United States Monument was a simple rectangular slab carved with high-relief allegorical figures, while that at Château Thierry was a Neoclassical temple form guarded by a massive stylized eagle behind a symbolic rendering of the Stars and Stripes.

War memorials in France, Germany, Italy and England abounded, with many French examples designed by or made with the participation of some of that country's premier Art Deco sculptors. Notable memorials included those at Aisne, Reims and Nice. In Italy the belated realization of a visionary Antonio Saint'Elia design, the 1933 War Memorial at Como, was undertaken under the direction of Giuseppe Terragni, while in London Charles Sargeant Jagger's Artillery Monument at Hyde Park Corner conveyed a highly idealized, yet very human, spirit of camaraderie and conflict in its bas-reliefs of soldiers.

Even cemeteries contained gravestones, mausoleums and other structures in the Art Deco style. In 1934, R. Berger designed additions for the 1820 Passy cemetery in Paris: a stone entrance with a Moderne-metalwork gate and a stone pavilion decorated with bas-reliefs by Janthial. The gate comprised rows of zigzag bands, and a plaque with the word 'PA ' in a contemporary typeface appeared at the top. In Cavtat, near Ragusa, Czechoslovakia, the octagon, cruciform-plan Racic Mortuary Chapel (Ivan Mestrovic, 1920–22) presented a bold modern face using local and traditional elements. Mestrovic, a Croatian sculptor-architect, had studied in Vienna, and the pair of monumental angel caryatids flanking the entrance to the stone and marble chapel, as well as the bronze one atop the cupola dome, owed a debt to Secession buildings.

One of the finest Moderne churches in the United States was Tulsa's Boston Avenue Methodist Church (*opposite*), its façade decorated with sculpture and topped by parapets and pinnacles. The elaborate sculptural embellishments of the 1928 church were the work of artist-teacher Adah Robinson, whose student, Bruce Goff (later one of the oil-rich city's most prominent architects), is credited with the design of the main structure. Moderne arches, stars, regional flora and praying hands were some of the symbols used – all were seen by Pastor John A. Rice as relevant to American Christianity.

Rationalist-classicist Auguste Perret's ecclesiastical architecture in France was based on traditional forms, but the exteriors were made up of innovative materials and sported, not the usual figural sculpture, but unusual abstract/symbolic designs. The façade of his 1922–23 church at Le Raincy (*right*) resembled a giant gameboard (the mesh-like elements were prefabricated).

Following along the lines of the Grundtvig Church was Barry Byrne's Christ the King in Cork, Ireland (*above*), dating from 1927-31, and one of the finest Moderne churches in the British Isles. It includes a sculpture of Christ by John Storrs.

A highly influential ecclesiastical structure was P.V. Jensen-Klint's Grundtvig Church in Copenhagen (*right*), begun in 1918 and completed in 1940 (Kaare Klint took over the project on his father's death in 1930).

The neo-Romanesque church of Sacre-Coeur at Gentilly outside Paris (*opposite left*), dating from 1931-36, included a quartet of attractive praying angels high atop its tower and a quasi-Moderne tympanum by sculptor Georges Saupique (*opposite below right*). Another dramatic tympanum, by sculptor Carlo Sarrabezolles (*opposite above right*), enriched the small church at Elisabethville, France, designed by Paul Tournon.

202

A spectacular finished project by Robert B. Stacy-Judd was the First Baptist Church in Ventura, California (*above*) of 1929-30; its stepped-pyramid central section recalled both Mayan ziggurats and the Grundtvig Church (see page 201). Most of his projects were never realized, such as the Philosophical Research Society in Los Angeles (*below*).

The forms of Moderne churches in North America ranged from classically inspired piles, such as the *c.*1931 Mormon Temple in Cardston, Alberta, Canada (*below*), to dramatic hybrids such as the Spanish Colonial Revival-cum-Art Deco Our Lady of Lourdes Roman Catholic Church in Los Angeles (*above*), designed by Lester G. Scherer. A forerunner of sorts to today's television ministry cathedrals was the 1933 Shrine of the Little Flower in Royal Oak, Michigan (*left above*), whose pastor, the Rev. Charles E. Coughlin, broadcast a popular radio programme from the Charity Crucifixion Tower (seen at left), which was sculpted by René Paul Chambellan.

Towering monuments of stone in the twenties and thirties, largely memorials to the fallen of the First World War, rose throughout Europe and the United States, and many included Moderne sculptures on their forms. In France, Marcel Loyan created the monument to the French artillery, the Crapouillots, on the plateau at Laffaux in Aisne (*opposite left*), and in Kansas City the huge 1921-26 Liberty Memorial complex (*opposite right*) was created by Harold Van Buren Magonigle, with Thomas and William Wight its architects. The stone pillar included figures of Courage, Hope, Patriotism and Sacrifice carved towards its crown, and ancillary structures included fountains and friezes honouring 'those who have dared bear the torches of sacrifice'. In Houston, the 570-feet high San Jacinto Monument (1938) (*right*), topped by a three-dimensional symbol of the Lone Star State, was for years the tallest such structure in the world.

The Anzac Memorial in Sydney's Hyde Park (*above*) was unveiled in November 1934 as the official state shrine to the memory of Australian ex-servicemen. Designed by C. Bruce Dellit, the 100-feet-high red granite mass, its dome topped with a stepped pyramid, included sculptures by Rayner Hoff and an amber window containing the Anzac rising sun, a motif appearing on the badge of the Australian military forces. The massive domed Monument to the Revolution in Mexico City (*opposite left*) included Moderne sculptural groups at the four upper corners of its square, arched form. In Nice, a stunning memorial to the fallen of the First World War (*opposite right*) was situated in a niche carved into the cliffside rock. Dramatic relief sculptures by Alfred-Auguste Janniot and other Art Deco carvers were set in front of the monument and along the plaza in front of it.

Chapter 6

Revivals and Replicas

In the City of London, Renton Howard Wood Levin Partnership's One America Square (*opposite*) incorporated an entrance area largely derived from Manhattan Moderne skyscrapers, with a glance towards British Odeons. Features include a shiny metal 'marquee', stepped-diamond parapet and sheer glass tower rising above the building's fifteen storeys. The largely rectilinear, granite-clad pile, which opened in 1991, is punctuated with zigzag bands and cylindrical forms.

In Miami Beach, the 1989 municipal parking garage (*below*), designed by Frankel & Associates, is unmistakably contemporary yet nicely sympathetic with the Art Deco confections in its midst. The area on which it was built had long been a parking lot and no thirties treasure was demolished to construct it.

From the early nineteen-seventies Art Deco as a decorative-arts and architectural style began to be recognized widely – and thus commenced its renaissance and recycling. Indeed, five decades on from the heyday of *le style moderne* (fifty years appearing to be the usual time lapse between a style's peak and revival), it seems a natural progression that numerous architects should recognize the beauty and high points of Art Deco buildings and duly echo or evoke some of their salient features in contemporary commissions. Michael Graves, Terry Farrell, Robert Venturi and Helmut Jahn, among others, have designed public buildings of Art Deco inspiration in the United States, Britain and Germany.

Graves (b.1934) has acknowledged his debt to Art Deco in several of his projects, including the Public Services Building in Portland, Oregon (1980-82). The towering Bank of the South West in Houston (1982), by German-born Jahn (b.1940) of Chicago-based Murphy/Jahn, is a glass skyscraper that has been termed 'Popular Machinism' by the architect himself, but is more appropriately described by the architectural historian Kenneth Frampton as 'neo-Art Deco' rendered as a 'giant Wurlitzer organ'. Other Jahn projects of note are One Liberty Place in Philadelphia (1986), its nocturnal silhouette, complete with zigzag neon at the top, likening it to a Post-Modern Chrysler Building, and Frankfurt's MesseTurm (1990), a towering, pyramid-capped marble and glass structure. In London, One America Square (Renton Howard Wood Levin Partnership, 1991) has an entryway of shiny metal and glass that evokes both New York skyscrapers and Oliver P. Bernard's entrance to the Strand Palace Hotel. Skidmore, Owings & Merrill's Worldwide Plaza in New York, with its stepped profile and eight-sided pyramidal top, is a comfortable throwback to the nineteen-twenties and thirties Manhattan skyscraper.

Other buildings do not echo thirties architecture per se but, rather, take their inspiration from other objects of the period. For instance, Shin Takamatsu's 1983 Kyoto dental surgery, the Ark, seems related to a thirties locomotive, though it is a far sturdier and loftier structure than a metal-clad American diner, which also had its design roots in trains. Even in the Miami Beach Historic District, where authentic Art Deco buildings are numerous, the 1989 multi-storey municipal parking garage in Collins Avenue (designed by Frankel & Associates) is a pink and white confection that comfortably coexists with its period neighbours.

A longtime, widescale 'adaptive use' of Art Deco architecture has been made in films and the fine and decorative arts. Indeed, ever since the years when Manhattan's skyscrapers began to define that city's silhouette, Hollywood film makers have been fascinated by the height, shape and decoration of these buildings. Everyone knows about *King Kong* (1933) and his travails on the Empire State, but Los Angeles' Bullock's Wilshire building figured in *The Big Sleep* (1946), and that same city's Eastern Columbia Building recently appeared in *Predator 2* (1991); its clock tower served as an arresting backdrop in promotional material for the film, indeed almost upstaging the eponymous star-alien. One of Frank Lloyd Wright's southern California textile-block residences, Milliard House, was used as a set for a party in *She* (1935), and no less than five models of the Chrysler Building featured as the far-off, fugitive Emerald City in *The Wiz* (1978), Sidney Lumet's black-cast remake of *The Wizard of Oz*; the film's production designer was Tony Walton, a longtime Art Deco devotee.

A number of films and plays which have featured visionary Art Deco-style buildings, from Fritz Lang's 1926 silent classic *Metropolis*, with its dizzying, claustrophobic mass of skyscrapers, to Frank Capra's *Lost Horizon* (1937), where the lamasery of Shangri-La was a Streamline Moderne Utopia, to David Butler's *Just Imagine* of 1930, whose vision of New York was, according to its designer, Stephen Goosson, inspired by Le Corbusier. In fact, the huge miniature set was closer in form and spirit to the visionary skyscrapers drawn by Hugh Ferriss in *The Metropolis of Tomorrow*, a collection of beautiful, highly influential renderings first published in 1929.

Dozens of films made use of skyscraper-inspired sets and even costumes, sometimes in amusingly inspired, inventive ways. Many stars' promotional photographs were taken against a *faux*-skyscraper backdrop. The films *Broadway* (1929), *Child of Manhattan* (1933), *42nd Street* (1933), *Broadway Melody of 1936* and *Broadway Melody of 1938* all featured dramatic backdrops of skyscraper-strewn skylines. Some were intended as authentic portraits of the city, while others were visionary. *Child of Manhattan* drew its images directly from Hugh Ferriss, for example; *Broadway* even includes a chorus line of 'skyscraperettes' wearing architectonic headdresses! Cedric Gibbons and Merrill Pye's fashion-show set for *Our Blushing Brides* (1930) comprised a huge obelisk fountain flanked by ornate grillework, very much in the Gallic mode. Parisian architect-designer Robert Mallet-Stevens in fact designed some sets for *L'Inhumaine* (1924), the earliest film to make use of modern architecture.

Art Deco buildings – real, but mostly imagined – were also the subject or inspiration for many paintings, sculptures, objects, and ephemeral and souvenir items in the nineteen-twenties and thirties (and indeed since the nineteen-seventies revival of interest in the style as well). For instance, there were souvenir green-enamelled-metal powder compacts from the Empire State Building that came in a stepped shape and featured incised geometric designs on the base-metal interior. Plastic-cased Air-King radios, designed by Harold van Doren and John Gordon Rideout around 1933, had a similar

Numerous designs – from furniture to buildings – by American architect Michael Graves have been informed by Art Deco (as well as Classicism), resulting in lively, colourful Post-Modern confections. The 1980-82 Portland Public Service Building (*above*), in Portland, Oregon, is basically a giant symmetrical cube, its façade enhanced by, among other elements, a garland of metallic ribbons – in effect, an update of the ornamental spandrels that adorned many Art Deco skyscrapers.

In Atlanta's High Museum of Art, Richard Meier took as his primary inspiration Le Corbusier's pure Modernism, but the 1980-83 structure also evoked the white-washed, multi-curved Streamline Moderne branch of Art Deco.

Some recent buildings do not so much echo Art Deco architecture as take their inspiration from other period objects, such as Shin Takamatsu's late eighties homage to industrial design: his gleaming, dramatically different Ark, a Kyoto dental surgery, evokes thirties locomotives (though it is a far loftier structure than a thirties American diner, which also had its roots in trains).

shape, and were available in bright red and lavender. Joseph Sinel's step-on scale for International Scale Corporation, *c.*1927, had a stepped silhouette, smart lettering and other Moderne motifs. The souvenirs available from the 1939 New York World Fair – some 900 manufacturers were licensed to produce over 25,000 items – presented the Trylon and Perisphere in myriad guises, materials and colours: as blue-and-orange or blue-and-white plastic salt and pepper shakers; in the centre of a lavender-hued commemorative plate (designed by Charles Murphy and made by the Homer Laughlin Company); as a frosted-glass table lamp-sculpture; enamelled in yellow on a brass license-plate attachment (for official use only); and painted on rather un-Moderne-looking oval-backed kitchen chairs of wood. A set of twelve silver-plated commemorative spoons was made by the William Rogers Manufacturing Company of Connecticut, each bowl featuring a different fair pavilion, with Trylon and Perisphere at the top of each handle.

Art Deco architecture-inspired objects also included high-priced, deluxe items. A rather impressionistic interpretation of New York in metal was Erik Magnussen's elegant burnished- and gilded-silver tea and coffee service, called 'The Lights and Shadows of Manhattan', made by Gorham in 1927. Many vastly different architectonic furniture forms of Art Deco inspiration were created by prominent designers of the day: for example, Kem Weber's tall Streamline Moderne wood and metal side table (1928-29) and Paul T. Frankl's sturdy and eminently practical wooden 'skyscraper' bookcases, cabinets and desks of the late twenties.

Contemporary artists and sculptors have also produced images of Art Deco, with elements of the architecture informing such disparate endeavours as children's toys (three-dimensional models and robots) and advertising campaigns (for Absolut Vodka in 1991, wherein the words 'Absolut Miami' appeared below an Absolut-bottle-shaped cream, pink and green confection of an Art Deco building). Michael Graves's 'Plaza' dressing table of 1981, for Memphis of Milan, was a three-dimensional fantasy (but a usable one) intended to be a replica of both building and man. Frank Siciliano's eighties 'Manhattan Suite' – ten conference chairs carved of solid cherrywood, their details then hand-painted with automobile metallic lacquer – paid sturdy homage to Manhattan buildings (each weighs some 150 pounds). Native New Yorker Paul Schulze's 1984 Steuben Glass sculpture, *New York, New York*, comprised 'shimmering evocations' of the Chrysler and Empire State buildings (as well as the Woolworth Building and twin towers of the World Trade Center) cut into the vertical edges of a crystal column.

Indeed, from the evidence in film and the decorative arts of the potency of Art Deco architectural imagery, from the soaring skyscraper to the suburban cinema, from the Paris 1925 pavilion to the chrome-sheathed highway diner, it is clear that many of these disparate Art Deco buildings possess a unique fascination for us. Whether they exist today as handsomely maintained or sadly derelict structures, or as photographic images only, they continue to possess an evocative power that will perhaps one day prove to be timeless.

One of the blue-glass-sheathed towers of Liberty Place in Philadelphia (*opposite*) by Helmut Jahn of the Chicago firm Murphy/Jahn pays homage to the Chrysler Building (at night it sports zigzags of neon); this massive complex dates from 1986. Skidmore, Owings & Merrill's subtly stepped Worldwide Plaza (*left*) dramatically evokes the massive stone piles of the twenties and thirties. In Louisville, Kentucky, Michael Graves's 1982-85 Humana Building (*above*) adheres to the basic tripartite building formula of the Art Deco skyscraper (base, shaft and ornamented crown) but is unmistakably Post-Modern; associate architects on the project were John Carl Warnecke and Associates.

One of Hollywood's most imaginative uses of the Art Deco skyscraper motif was in Paul Fejos's 1929 film, *Broadway*; its art director was Charles D. Hall, whose elaborate nightclub set included stunning backdrops of looming skyscrapers and architectonic standard lamps, but the *tour-de-force* of the film was the apparel of the 'skyscraperette' dancers (*above*). The silhouettes of Moderne skyscrapers were reproduced by both sculptures and neon lights in this backdrop (*right*) for MGM's extravaganza, *Broadway Melody of 1938*, directed by Roy del Ruth in 1937.

Shangri La's lamasery in Frank Capra's 1937 *Lost Horizon* (*above*) was a Streamline Moderne Utopia with a handful of high-style Parisian decorative elements (supervisory art director was Stephen Goosson), while Fritz Lang's 1926 *Metropolis* (*opposite centre*) was set in a sinister, monstrous maze of skyscrapers; its art directors were Otto Hunte, Erich Kettelhut and Karl Vollbrecht. On lighter notes, Ruby Keeler danced up a stairway flanked by jaunty Deco towers in Lloyd Bacon's 1933 *42nd Street* (*opposite below*), art-directed by Jack Okey and choreographed by Busby

Berkeley, while Michael Jackson and Diana Ross 'eased on down' the Yellow Brick Road to an Emerald City of five Chrysler Buildings (*right above*) in Sidney Lumet's 1978 film musical *The Wiz*. Illustrated here is production designer Tony Walton's sketch for the elaborate set.

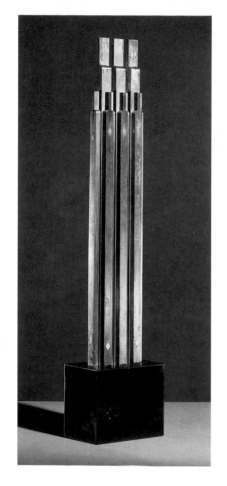

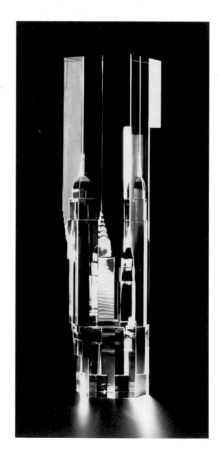

A wide range of sculpture, furniture and other decorative art objects in the twenties and thirties – and in the more recent past as well – have paid homage to Art Deco architecture. John Storrs (see also page 201) created his bronze sculpture 'New York' (*opposite below left*) around 1925, while Steuben Glass designer Paul Schulze's homage to his native city, 'New York, New York' (*opposite below centre*), was introduced by Steuben in 1984; its four-part 'urban panorama' includes not only the Chrysler, Empire State and Woolworth buildings, but also the World Trade Center. Its top that of a futuristic skyscraper, the emerald-studded silver cocktail shaker by Tiffany and Company (*opposite above left*) was exhibited, along with the rest of the cocktail service, in The House of Jewels at the 1939 New York World Fair.

Furniture inspired by Art Deco buildings included a pair of sturdy wooden 'skyscraper' chest of drawers by New York interior and furniture designer Paul Theodore Frankl (*above right*) and Californian Kem Weber's jazzy 1928-29 wood and metal side table (*opposite right*), one of several pieces designed for Mr and Mrs John Bissinger of San Francisco; its silvered and painted surfaces, and especially its two architectonic side lamps, give it a fantastic Hollywood-Deco aura. The architectonic forms of the copper bookends (*below right*), probably designed by Karl Kipp for Roycroft Copper and made in c.1915-22, are quite simple, yet nonetheless presage the exuberant geometric forms and zigzags of Art Deco.

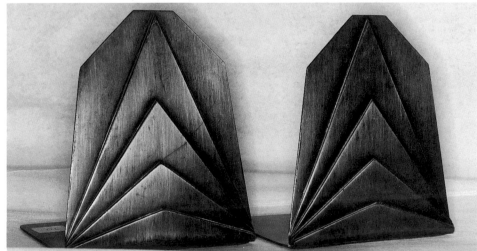

Illustration Credits

Agence T.O.P., Paris: 11 (top right; photo Joel Ducange), 35 (bottom; photo © Marc Tulane), 70–1 (bottom; photo Joel Ducange), 151 (Joel Ducange) 162 (photo Daniel Bouquignaud). © T. & R. Annan & Sons Ltd., Glasgow: 28 (top right). Architectural Association Slide Library, London: 131 (right). © *Architectural Review*: 34 (top). Courtesy Arizona Biltmore, Phoenix: 82 (left). Courtesy Arrasmith, Judd, Rapp, Inc., Louisville, KY: 172 (top and middle). Atlantic Richfield Co., Corporate Archives: 104 (right). Australian Overseas Information Service, London: 206. Australian Tourist Commission: 62 (bottom left). Collection Patricia Bayer: 1, 42, 50 (bottom), 51 (all photos by Eileen Tweedy), 54 (bottom left and right, photos by Eileen Tweedy), 55 (top and middle), 84, 100 (bottom), 118 (bottom right), 127 (middle), 148 (bottom), 171 (top; photo by Eileen Tweedy), 179 (left), 183 (two middle and bottom), 203 (top left), 207 (left), 219 (bottom; courtesy The Elbert Hubbard Foundation, East Aurora, NY). Photos by Patricia Bayer: 6, 10 (top right, middle left, middle right, bottom left), 11 (top left, middle right, bottom left, bottom right), 63 (top left and bottom), 66 (top and bottom), 70 (top and bottom), 71 (top and right), 74, 78 (all), 79 (all), 90 (top left and bottom), 91 (bottom), 106 (top), 111 (top), 122 (top left), 135 (both), 138 (bottom left), 158–9 (top), 163 (middle), 170, 171 (bottom), 178, 186 (left, right top and middle), 209, 212, 213 (left). Courtesy Best Products, Richmond, VA: 174 (bottom; photo by Norman McGrath). The Bettmann Archive Inc., New York: 52 (top), 53 (both; UPI/Bettmann), 64 (bottom left), 69 (bottom; UPI/Bettmann), 73 (right; UPI/Bettmann), 104 (left), 96 (UPI/Bettmann), 124 (bottom; UPI/Bettmann), 131 (right), 133 (right bottom; UPI/Bettmann), 164 (top left), 174 (top), 180 (top), 181, 188 (left), 191 (both), 205. © Bildarchiv d. Öst. Nationalbibliothek, Vienna: 27 (top right). © British Architectural Library/RIBA: 69 (top). Photo Richard Bryant, Architectural Photography and Picture Library: 59. Bureau of Reclamation, U.S. Department of the Interior: 189 (both). © Central Electricity Generating Board: 124 (top). Compliments of Chevron Corporation: 168 (bottom). © City of Liverpool, City Engineers Dept.: 184–5 (middle), 188 (top right). Courtesy of the Cooper-Hewitt Museum, The Smithsonian Institution's National Museum of Design: 109. Cosmos Images, Napier, New Zealand: 58 (right), 75 (top left), 111 (bottom). Photos by David Coultas, London: 82 (right top and bottom), 83. Courtesy Design Analysis International Ltd., London/Shin Takamatsu/Kyoto: 211 (bottom). Alastair Duncan: 90 (right), 108 (left; photo Scott Hyde), 218 (right; collection George Waterman III); 219 (top; collection John P. Axelrod). Edifice/Darley: 10 (top left), 63 (top right), 127 (top), 179 (right); Edifice/Knott: 35 (top right), 118 (top); Edifice/Lewis; 75 (right), 139 (bottom right), 163 (bottom). Edimédia, Paris: 35 (top left; photo P. Hinous), 67 (© Photo J. Guillot, *Connaissance des Arts*). Photos by Robert Estall: 122 (bottom left). © Esto/Ezra Stoller: 211 (top). Photos by Allen Eyles: 2, 70 (middle), 90 (top), 102 (bottom), 139 (top), 154–5 (middle), 155 (right), 158 (left), 159 (right), 163 (top). Courtesy Ford Motor Co. Ltd. 9 (top). © Frank Lloyd Wright Foundation: 28 (top left). © Michael Freeman: 11 (middle left), 126 (top). Photos by Barbara Friedland, New York: 10 (bottom right), 134 (bottom), 140, 141, 154 (left), 158–9 (bottom), 186 (bottom right), 187. © Photo by Yukio Futagawa: 100 (top). Galerie Moderne, London: 68 (all; photos by Eileen Tweedy). Michael Graves, Princeton: 210 (Proto Acme Photo), 213 (right; photo by Paschall/Taylor). Greater London Photograph Library: 88, 142 (top left), 149 (top right), 152 (top right and bottom), 160 (top), 177, 193. Photo by Max R. Hagemann: 117. Courtesy Historical Association of Southern Florida, Miami News Collection: 131 (bottom left). © Angelo Hornak, London: 86, 94 (all), 95, 103, 107, 115, 122 (right), 123, 126 (bottom). Courtesy Indianapolis Museum of Art: 218 (bottom left; photo by Robert Wallace). © Randy Juster, San Mateo, CA: 93, 102 (top), 106 (bottom), 118 (bottom left), 127 (bottom), 150 (both), 175 (both), 183 (top). Courtesy The Landmark Society of Western New York, Rochester: 114 (photo by Hans Padelt). © London Transport Board: 112 (bottom), 173 (all). Courtesy London Zoo, © Zoo Operations Ltd.: 185 (top). Courtesy The Maybury, Edinburgh: 134. Courtesy Museum of Contemporary Art, Sydney: 110. Courtesy The Museum of Modern Art, New York: 34 (bottom left). Courtesy Museum of the City of New York: 13. National Audit Office, London: 172 (bottom left: photo © Nik Bartrum). Nederlands Architectuurinstituut, Amsterdam: 25 (bottom left and right), 31 (top). Photo by Peter Olson, Philadelphia: 12 (top). Courtesy One America Square Properties Ltd., London: 208 (photograph © Terry Hardy). Photo by Gareth O'Sullivan, Cork: 201 (left). Photofest, New York: 36, 48, 49 (bottom), 54 (top left), 55 (bottom), 105, 112 (top), 180 (bottom), 214, 215, 216, 217 (middle and bottom). © Plansammlung der Universitätsbibliothek der Technischen Universität Berlin: 28 (bottom). Roger-Viollet, Paris: 26 (top left), 26–7 (bottom middle), 30 (bottom right), 40, 46 (top; © ND-Viollet), 46 (middle; photo Branger-Viollet), 46 (bottom; © Roger-Viollet), 47 (top left; © Harlingue-Viollet), 47 (top right; © LL-Viollet), 47 (middle right; © Branger-Viollet), 47 (bottom; © LL-Viollet), 72, 73 (top left; © Roger-Viollet), 73 (bottom left; © Collection Viollet), 77 (© Collection Viollet), 132 (top; Harlingue-Viollet), 132 (bottom right), 133 (top right), 148 (top), 149 (left), 149 (bottom right; © Roger-Viollet), 152 (top left; © Roger-Viollet), 160 (bottom; © CAP-Viollet), 161 (bottom; © CAP-Viollet), 164 (bottom left; © CAP-Viollet), 164 (right; © Roger-Viollet), 165 (top; © Roger-Viollet), 165 (bottom left; © Harlingue-Viollet), 185 (bottom; © Harlingue-Viollet), 199, 200 (left), 200 (bottom right; © Collection Viollet), 204 (left; © Harlingue-Viollet), 207 (right). © Sandak Inc., Stamford, CT: 35 (bottom right), 101. © Julius Shulman, Los Angeles: 56, 64 (top), 65 (both), 129, 136 (top), 153, 184 (top). © John Sims: 15. Photo courtesy Steuben, New York: 218 (bottom middle). © Dr Franz Stoedtner/Heinz Klemm, Düsseldorf: 27 (bottom right), 29 (both), 30 (top left and top right). Photos by Jessica Strang, London: 62 (bottom right), 182. © Tim Stuart, Dublin: 119, 138. © Curt Teich Postcard Archives, Lake County (IL) Museum: 58 (top left), 165 (bottom right). Thames and Hudson archive: 9 (bottom), 12 (bottom), 24 (both), 25 (top), 26 (bottom left), 26–7 (top middle), 30 (bottom left), 31 (bottom), 32 (all), 33 (all), 96, 99 (bottom left), 108 (right), 130 (top left), 131 (top left), 143 (bottom), 145, 161 (top), 184 (bottom), 197, 204 (right). Courtesy Tiffany & Co.: 218 (top left). Tokyo Metropolitan Teien Art Museum: 62 (top). Photos by Eileen Tweedy, London: 14, 21, 49 (top), 50 (top and middle), 52 (bottom), 58 (bottom left), 60, 64 (bottom right), 99 (right), 125 (all), 130 (bottom), 137 (right), 142, 143 (top right), 188 (bottom right), 192, 200 (top right), 201 (right), 203 (top right and bottom). © Twentieth Century Fox: 99 (top left; photo by Richard Foreman). University of California, Santa Barbara, Architectural Drawing Collection/University Art Museum: 85, 113, 132 (bottom left), 133 (left; photo by David Gebhard), 136 (bottom), 168 (top; photo by David Gebhard), 202 (both). Courtesy Tony Walton: 217 (top). Photo by Bob Warburton, Blackpool: 74 (bottom left).

Bibliography

The following titles represent but a selection of the myriad books, guides and pamphlets of both the distant and recent past written about or including various aspects of Art Deco/Moderne architecture and its creators and patrons, as well as its predecessors, influences, contemporaries and successors.

Adam, Peter, *Eileen Gray Architect/Designer, A Biography*, London and New York, 1987.

Albrecht, Donald, *Designing Dreams: Modern Architecture in the Movies*, New York, 1986; London, 1987.

Alleman, Robert, *The Movie Lover's Guide to Hollywood*, New York, 1986.

Appelbaum, Stanley, *The New York World's Fair 1930/1940 in Photographs by Richard Wurts and Others*, New York, 1977.

Arts Council of Great Britain, *Thirties, British Art and Design before the War*, London, 1979.

Arwas, Victor, *Art Deco*, London and New York, 1980.

Atwell, David, *Cathedrals of the Movies*, London, 1980.

Bader, John, *Diners*, New York, 1978.

Balfour, Alan, *Rockefeller Center, Architecture as Theatre*, New York, 1978.

Battersby, Martin, *The Decorative Twenties*, London and New York, 1969 (reprinted 1989).

Battersby, Martin, *The Decorative Thirties*, London and New York, 1971 (reprinted 1989).

Baxter, John, *The Australian Cinema*, Sydney, 1970.

Bayer, Patricia, *Art Deco Source Book*, Oxford and New York, 1988.

Bel Geddes, Norman, *Horizons*, Boston, 1932.

Binney, Marcus; Machin, Francis and Powell, Ken, *Bright Future, The Re-use of Industrial Buildings*, London, 1990.

Borghini, Sandro; Salama, Hugo and Solsona, Justo, *1930–1950 Arquitectura Moderna en Buenos Aires*, Buenos Aires, 1987.

Borsi, Franco, *The Monumental Era, European Architecture and Design 1929–1939*, London, 1987.

Bossom, Alfred, *Building to the Sky: The Romance of the Skyscraper*, London, 1934.

Breeze, Carla, *L.A. Deco*, New York, 1991.

Breeze, Carla, *Pueblo Deco*, New York, 1990.

Brown, Robert K., *Art Deco Internationale*, New York and London, 1977.

Brumfield, W.C., *The Origins of Modernism in Russian Architecture*, Berkeley, California, 1991.

Brunhammer, Yvonne, *The Art Deco Style*, London, 1983; New York, 1984.

Brunhammer, Yvonne, *Cinquantenaire de l'Exposition de 1925*, Paris, 1976.

Buchanan, Richard (ed.), *Mackintosh's Masterwork, The Glasgow School of Art*, Glasgow, 1989.

Bush, Donald J., *The Streamlined Decade*, New York, 1975.

Cabanne, Pierre, *Encyclopédie Art Deco*, Paris, 1986.

Capitman, Barbara Baer, *Deco Delights*, New York, 1988.

Capitman, Barbara Baer (ed.), *Portfolio: The Architecture and Design of Miami Beach*, New York, 1981.

Cerwinske, Laura, *Tropical Deco: The Architecture and Design of Old Miami Beach*, New York, 1981.

Chanin, Irwin S., *A Romance with the City*, New York, 1982.

Coe, Peter and Reading, Malcolm, *Lubektin & Tecton, An Architectural Study*, London, 1991.

Cohen, Judith Singer, *Cowtown Moderne: Art Deco Architecture of Fort Worth, Texas*, College Station, Texas, 1988.

Cook, Catherine and Ageros, Justin (eds.), *Architectural Design Profiles 93: The Avant-Garde, Russian Architecture in the Twenties*, 1991.

Cooper, Jackie (ed.), *Mackintosh Architecture*, London, 1977; New York, 1984.

Copplestone, Trewin, *Twentieth-Century World Architecture*, London, 1991.

Corn, Joseph J. and Horrigan, Brian, *Yesterday's Tomorrows: Past Visions of the American Future*, New York, 1984.

Country Life, *Recent English Architecture 1920–1940*, London, 1947.

Cox, Warren J.; Jacobsen, Hugh Newell et al., *A Guide to the Architecture of Washington, D.C.*, New York, 1974.

Cucchiella, Sheryl R., *Baltimore Deco: An Architectural Survey of Art Deco in Baltimore*, Baltimore, 1984.

Cuffley, Peter, *Australian Houses of the '20s & '30s*, Fitzroy, Victoria, 1989.

Curtis, William J.R., *Modern Architecture since 1900*, Oxford, 1982.

Dean, David, *Architecture of the 1930s, Recalling the English Scene*, New York, 1983.

Delorme, Jean Claude and Chair, Philippe, *L'Ecole de Paris, 10 architectes et leurs immeubles, 1905–1937*, Paris, 1981.

Deshoulières, Dominique and Jeanneau, Hubert (eds.), *Rob. Mallet-Stevens: Architecte*, Brussels, 1980.

Detroit Institute of Arts, *The Legacy of Albert Kahn*, Detroit, 1970.

de Wit, Wim (gen. ed.), *The Amsterdam School, Dutch Expressionist Architecture, 1915–1930*, New York and Cambridge, Massachusetts, 1983.

De Witt, Dennis J. and Elizabeth R., *Modern Architecture in Europe, A Guide to Buildings since the Industrial Revolution*, London, 1987.

Duncan, Alastair, *American Art Deco*, London and New York, 1986.

Duncan, Alastair, *Art Deco*, London, 1988.

Etlin, R.A., *Modernism in Italian Architecture, 1890–1940*, Cambridge, Massachusetts, 1991.

Eyles, Allen and Skone, Keith, *London's West End Cinemas*, Sutton, London, 1991.

Ferriss, Hugh, *The Metropolis of Tomorrow*, New York, 1929 (reprinted 1986).

Field, Audrey, *Picture Palace: A Social History of the Cinema*, London, 1974.

Ford, James and Ford, Katherine Morrow, *Classic Modern Homes of the Thirties*, New York, *c.*1940 (reprinted 1989).

Foundation for Architecture, *Philadelphia Architecture, A Guide to the City*, Philadelphia, 1984.

Frampton, Kenneth, *Modern Architecture, A Critical History*, London, 1985.

Frankl, Paul T., *New Dimensions*, New York, 1928.

Frankl, Paul T., *Form and Re-Form*, New York, 1930.

Friedman, Mildred (ed.), *De Stijl: 1917–1931 Visions of Utopia*, Oxford, 1982.

Gebhard, David; Sandweiss, Eric and Winter, Robert, *Architecture in San Francisco and Northern California*, Salt Lake City, 1976 (revised edition).

Gebhard, David and Von Breton, Harriette, *Kem Weber: The Moderne in Southern California, 1920–1941*, Santa Barbara, 1969.

Gebhard, David and Von Breton, Harriette, *L.A. in the Thirties, 1931–1941*, Salt Lake City, 1975.

Gebhard, David and Winter, Robert, *Architecture in Los Angeles, A Compleat Guide*, Salt Lake City, 1985.

Gebhard, David and Zimmerman, Kurt, *The California Architecture of Frank Lloyd Wright*, San Francisco, 1988; London, 1989.

Glory, June, *Art Deco in Indianapolis*, Indianapolis, 1980.

Goldberger, Paul, *The City Observed: New York, A Guide to the Architecture of Manhattan*, New York, 1979.

Goldberger, Paul, *The Skyscraper*, New York, 1982.

Gould, Jeremy, *Modern Houses in Britain 1919–1939*, London, 1977.

Greenberg, Cara (ed.), *1975 New York Art Deco Exposition at Radio City Music Hall*, New York, 1975.

Greif, Martin, *Depression Modern: The Thirties Style in America*, New York, 1975.

Gutman, Richard J.S. and Kaufman, Elliott, *American Diner*, New York, 1979.

Hall, Ben M., *The Best Remaining Seats: The Story of the Golden Age of the Movie Palace*, New York, 1961.

Handlin, David P., *American Architecture*, London, 1985.

Hanks, David, *The Decorative Designs of Frank Lloyd Wright*, New York, 1979.

Harrison, Helen A., *Dawn of a New Day: The New York World's Fair, 1939–40*, New York, 1980.

Hatton, Hay, *Tropical Splendor: An Architectural History of Florida*, New York, 1987.

Hausen, M. and Mikkola, K., *Eliel Saarinen Projects 1896–1923*, Cambridge, Massachusetts, 1990.

Heide, Robert and Gilman, John, *Popular Art Deco, Depression Era Style and Design*, New York, 1991.

Henneke, Susan P. (ed.); Gebhard, David; Johnson, Carol N. et al., *Tulsa Art Deco: An Architectural Era, 1925–1942*, Tulsa, Oklahoma, 1980.

Hildebrand, Grant, *Designing for Industry: The Architecture of Albert Kahn*, Cambridge, Massachusetts, 1974.

Hillier, Bevis, *Art Deco of the 20s and 30s*, London and New York, 1968.

Hillier, Bevis, *The World of Art Deco*, New York, 1971.

Hirshorn, Paul and Izenour, Steve, *White Towers*, Cambridge, Massachusetts, 1979.

Hitchcock, Henry-Russell and Bauer, C., *Modern Architecture in England*, New York, 1937 (reprinted 1969).

Hitchcock, Henry-Russell and Johnson, Philip, *The International Style: Architecture since 1922*, New York, 1932 (reprinted).

Ingle, Marjorie I., *The Mayan Revival Style*, Salt Lake City, 1984.

James, Cary, *Frank Lloyd Wright's Imperial Hotel*, New York, 1968.

James, Theodore, Jr., *The Empire State Building*, New York, 1975.

Joedicke, Joachim Andreas, *Helmut Jahn, Design of a New Architecture*, Zürich, 1986.

Jones, D.W.K. and Davis, B.J., *Green Line 1930–1980*, London, 1980.

Jordy, William H., *American Buildings and Their Architects, the Impact of European Modernism in the Mid-Twentieth Century*, New York, 1972.

Kaplan, Donald and Bellink, Alan, *Classic Diners of the Northeast*, Boston and London, 1980.

Kaplan, Sam Hall, *L.A. Lost & Found, An Architectural History of Los Angeles*, New York, 1987.

Karol, Eitan and Allibone, Finch, *Charles Holden Architect 1875–1960*, Glasgow, 1985.

Kenna, Rudolph, *Glasgow Art Deco*, Glasgow, 1985.

Kilham, Walter H., *Raymond Hood, Architect*, New York, 1973.

Kingsbury, Martha, *Age of the Thirties–The Pacific Northwest*, Seattle, 1972.

Kittel, Gerd, *Diners, People and Places*, London, 1990.

Klein, Dan, *All Colour Book of Art Deco*, New York, 1974.

Klein, Dan; McClelland, Nancy A. and Haslam, Malcolm, *In the Deco Style*, New York, 1986; London, 1987.

Kreisman, Lawrence and Gardaya, Victor, *Art Deco Seattle*, Seattle, 1979.

Krinsky, Carol Herselle, *Rockefeller Center*, Oxford, London and New York, 1978.

Kuckro, Anne Crofoot, *Hartford Architecture, Volume One: Downtown Hartford*, Hartford, 1978.

Lacloche, Francis, *Architectures de Cinémas*, Paris, 1981.

Lampugnani, V.M. (gen. ed.), *The Thames and Hudson Encyclopaedia of 20th-Century Architecture*, London, 1986.

Latham, Ian (ed.), *New Free Style Arts and Crafts-Art Nouveau-Secession*, London, 1980.

Le Corbusier, *Towards a New Architecture (Vers une Architecture)*, Paris, 1923; London, 1927.

Leich, Jean Ferriss, *Architectural Visions, The Drawings of Hugh Ferriss*, New York, 1980.

Liebs, Chester H., *Main Street to Miracle Mile: American Roadside Architecture*, New York, 1985.

McGrath, Raymond, *Twentieth Century Houses*, London, 1934.

McGrath, Raymond and Frost, A.C., *Glass in Architecture and Decoration*, London, 1937 (reprinted 1961).

MacKertich, Tony and MacKertich, Peter, *Façade, A Decade of British and American Commercial Architecture*, London and New York, 1976.

Maenz, Paul, *Art Deco: 1920–1940*, Cologne, 1974.

Mandelbaum, Howard and Myers, Eric, *Screen Deco, A Celebration of High Style in Hollywood*, New York, 1985.

Margolies, John and Gwathmey, Emily, *Ticket to Paradise, American Movie Theaters and How We Had Fun*, Boston, 1991.

Martin, Hervé, *Guide de l'Architecture Moderne à Paris, 1900–1990*, Paris, 1987.

Mattie, Erik, *Amsterdam School*, Amsterdam, 1991.

Meikle, Jeffrey, *Twentieth-Century Limited: Industrial Design in America, 1925–1939*, Philadelphia, 1979.

Menten, Theodore, *The Art Deco Style in Household Objects, Architecture, Sculpture, Graphics, Jewelry*, New York, 1972.

Miller, Nory, *Helmut Jahn*, New York, 1986.

Mujica, Francisco, *History of the Skyscraper*, Paris, 1929 (reprinted 1977).

Musée des Arts Décoratifs, *Les Années "25", Art Déco/Bauhaus/Stijl/Esprit Nouveau*, Paris, 1966.

Naylor, David, *American Picture Palaces, The Architecture of Fantasy*, New York, 1981.

Naylor, David, *Great American Movie Theaters*, Washington, D.C., 1987.

Naylor, Gillian, *The Bauhaus*, London, 1968.

Nebehay, Christian M., *Vienna 1900, Architecture and Painting*, Vienna, 1988.

Neuhaus, Eugene, *The Art of Treasure Island*, Berkeley, California, 1939.

Nichols, Karen Vogel; Burke, Patrick J. and Hancock, Caroline (eds.), *Michael Graves: Buildings and Projects 1982–1989*, New York, 1990.

Norberg-Schulz, Christian, *Modern Norwegian Architecture*, Oslo, 1986.

Oliver, Richard, *Bertram Grosvenor Goodhue*, Cambridge, Massachusetts, 1983.

Overy, Paul, *De Stijl*, London, 1968.

Overy, Paul; Büller, Lenneke; den Oudsten, Frank and Mulder, Berthus, *The Rietveld-Schröder House*, Houten, 1988.

Parco, *Czechoslovakia Cubism: The World of Architecture, Furniture and Craft*, Tokyo, 1984.

Park, Marlene and Markowitz, Gerald E., *Democratic Vistas: Post Offices and Public Art in the New Deal*, Philadelphia, 1984.

Pevsner, Nikolaus, *The Sources of Modern Architecture and Design*, New York and London, 1968.

Pildas, Ave, *Art Deco Los Angeles*, New York, 1977.

Pildas, Ave and Smith, Lucinda, *Movie Palaces: Survivors of an Elegant Era*, New York, 1980.

Pilgrim, Dianne H.; Tashjian, Dickran and Wilson, Richard Guy *The Machine Age in America 1918–1941*, New York, 1986.

Pinchon, Jean-François, *Robert Mallet-Stevens*, Cambridge, Massachusetts, 1991.

Poulos, Arthur J., *American Design Ethic: A History of Industrial Design to 1940*, Cambridge, Massachusetts, 1983.

Quinan, Jack, *Frank Lloyd Wright's Larkin Building, Myth and Fact*, Cambridge, Massachusetts, and London, 1987.

Reinhardt, Richard, *Treasure Island: San Francisco's Exposition Years*, San Francisco, 1978.

Richards, Jeffrey, *The Age of the Dream Palace, Cinema and Society in Britain 1930–1939*, London, 1984.

Robinson, Cervin and Bletter, Rosemarie Haag, *Skyscraper Style: Art Deco New York*, New York, 1975.

Root, Keith, *Miami Beach Art Deco Guide*, Miami Beach, 1987.

Rothery, Sean, *Ireland and the New Architecture 1900–1940*, Dublin, 1991.

Sabbach, Karl, *Skyscraper, The Making of a Building*, London, 1989; New York, 1990.

Saliga, Pauline A. (ed.) et al., *The Sky's the Limit, A Century of Chicago Skyscrapers*, New York, 1990.

Scarlett, Frank and Townley, Marjorie, *Arts Décoratifs 1925: A Personal Recollection of the Paris Exhibition*, London and New York, 1975.

Schleier, Merrill, *The Skyscraper in American Art, 1890–1931*, New York, 1986.

Schweiger, Werner J., *Wiener Werkstätte, Design in Vienna 1903–1932*, London, 1984.

Sembach, Klaus-Jürgen, *Into the Thirties: Style and Design, 1927–1934*, London, 1972.

Sembach, Klaus-Jürgen, *Style 1930*, New York, 1971.

Sergeant, John and Mooring, Stephen (eds.), *Architectural Design Profiles 16: Bruce Goff*, London, 1978.

Sharp, Dennis, *The Picture Palace and Other Buildings for the Movies*, London and New York, 1969.

Sharp, Dennis, *Twentieth Century Architecture, A Visual History*, London, 1991.

Shaw, Peter and Hallett, Peter, *Art Deco Napier, Styles of the Thirties*, Napier, New Zealand, 1987.

Siegel, Arthur (ed.), *Chicago's Famous Buildings*, Chicago, 1969 (revised edition).

Spade, Rupert, *Eero Saarinen*, London and New York, 1971.

Stamp, Gavin (ed.), *Architectural Design Profiles 24: Britain in the Thirties*, London, n.d.

Stamp, Gavin, *A Celebration of 1930s Architecture, Paintings by Tabitha Salmon*, London, 1991.

Stern, Rudi, *Let There Be Neon*, New York, 1979.

Stone, Susannah Harris, *The Oakland Paramount*, Berkeley, California, 1982.

Storrer, William Allin, *The Architecture of Frank Lloyd Wright: A Complete Catalogue*, Cambridge, Massachusetts, 1979.

Striner, Richard (intro.), *Mostly Moderne, Views from America's Past*, Washington, D.C., 1989.

Sullivan, Donald G. and Danforth, Brian J., *Bronx Art Deco Architecture*, New York, 1976.

Teague, Walter Dorwin, *Design This Day, The Technique of Order in the Machine Age*, New York, 1940.

Thorne, Ross, *Picture Palace Architecture in Australia*, South Melbourne, 1976.

Tokyo Metropolitan Teien Art Museum, *The Building and Its History*, Tokyo, 1987.

University of Cincinnati, *Art Deco and the Cincinnati Union Terminal*, Cincinnati, 1973.

Valerio, Joseph M. and Friedman, Daniel, *Movie Palaces: Renaissance and Re-Use*, New York, 1982.

van Hoogstraten, Nicholas, *Lost Broadway Theatres*, New York, 1991.

Varian, Elayne H., *American Art Deco Architecture*, New York, 1974.

Varnedoe, Kirk, *Vienna 1900: Art, Architecture & Design*, New York, 1986.

Vellay, Marc and Frampton, Kenneth, *Pierre Chareau*, London, 1985.

Vieyra, Daniel K., *"Fill 'er Up": An Architectural History of America's Gas Stations*, New York, 1979.

Vlack, Don, *Art Deco Architecture in New York 1920–1940*, New York, 1974.

Wagner, Otto, *Moderne Architektur*, Vienna, 1896 (1902 edition reprinted as *Modern Architecture*, Santa Monica, California, 1988).

Weber, Eva, *Art Deco in America*, New York, 1985.

Wheeler, Karen Vogel; Arnell, Peter and Bickford, Ted (eds.), *Michael Graves: Buildings and Projects 1966–1981*, New York, 1983.

Whiffen, Marcus and Breeze, Carla, *Pueblo Deco: The Art Deco Architecture of the Southwest*, Albuquerque, New Mexico, 1983.

Whitford, Frank, *Bauhaus*, London, 1984.

Wilson, Richard Guy (intro.) et al., *Public Buildings, Architecture under the Public Works Administration, 1933–39, Vol. I* (reprinted New York, 1986).

Wingler, Hans M., *Bauhaus*, Cambridge, Massachusetts, 1969.

Wirz, Hans and Striner, Richard, *Washington Deco: Art Deco in the Nation's Capital*, Washington, D.C., 1984.

Wright, Frank Lloyd, *The Story of the Tower*, New York, 1956.

Yorke, F.R.S., *The Modern House*, London, 1934.

Zim, Larry; Lerner, Mel and Rolfes, Herb, *The World of Tomorrow: The 1939 New York World's Fair*, New York, 1988.

SELECTED GUIDE BOOKS TO WORLD FAIRS

Catalogue Général Officiel, Exposition Internationale des Arts Décoratifs et Industriels Modernes, Paris, 1925.

Official Guide Book of the Fair 1933, A Century of Progress, Chicago, 1933.

Album Officiel/Photographies en Couleur, Exposition Internationale des Arts et des Techniques Appliqués à la Vie Moderne, Paris, 1937.

Official Guide Book, New York World's Fair, The World of Tomorrow 1939, New York, 1939.

Official Souvenir, 1939 Golden Gate International Exposition, Treasure Island and the World's Greatest Spans of Steel, San Francisco, 1939.

Index of Buildings, Architects and Expositions Numbers in italics refer to illustrations

WCAU Building, Philadelphia 90, 93; *12, 91*
Weber, Karl Emanuel Martin (Kem) 76, 211, 219; *58, 218*
Webster Hotel, Miami Beach *82*
Weddell, James W. 84, 128; *75*
Weiss, Dreyfous & Seiferth 177; *180*
Welch & Lander 167
Welch, Cachemaille-Day & Lander 195

White Towers 140
'White Walls', Torquay 60
Will Rogers Memorial Auditorium, Coliseum and Tower, Fort Worth 42, 157, 182; *183*
Williams, E.A. 85, 97, 144; *111*
Williams, Sir E. Owen 84, 117, 195; *88*
Wiltern Theater, Los Angeles 147
Withers, Elmer G. 85, 177, 182; *183*

Withers, William Henry 97; *110–11*
Wiz, The 210; *217*
Wood, Edgar 18
Works Progress Administration 87, 190
World fairs (see Expositions)
Worldwide Plaza, New York 209; *213*
Wright, Eric Lloyd 58
Wright, Frank Lloyd 19, 20, 22, 29, 58, 76,

85, 97, 101, 120, 146, 157, 177, 182, 196, 210; *21, 28, 34, 59, 82, 96, 100*
Wright, Lloyd 76; *64*
Wright's Trading Post, Albuquerque 140; *141*
Wurdeman, Walter 156

ZINK, John J. 156
Zook, R. Harold 156

Index of Places   *Numbers in italics refer to illustrations*